Table of Contents

Background and Overview

This 2014 Measuring Broadband America Report on Fixed Broadband ("Report") contains the most recent data collected from fixed Internet Service Providers (ISPs) as part of the Federal Communication Commission's (FCC) Measuring Broadband America program. This program is an ongoing, rigorous, nationwide study of consumer broadband performance in the United States. We measure the network performance delivered to a representative sample set of the population and service tier demographics across the United States. The sample population is drawn from subscribers of ISPs serving over 80% of the residential marketplace, and consists of thousands of volunteers.

The initial Measuring Broadband America Report on Fixed Broadband was published in August 2011, and presented the first broad-scale study of directly measured consumer broadband performance throughout the United States. This effort was followed approximately one year later by a second Report, released in July 2012, a third Report released in February 2013, and now this Report. We intend to provide these reports going forward on an annual basis to serve as consistent benchmarks on the health of broadband Internet access services in the United States, and to better chart progress towards the FCC goal of continuing to evolve the speeds and quality of service at which broadband access is commonly available to the American public.

As explained in the accompanying Technical Appendix, each Report in this series is based on measurements taken during a single reference month that has been chosen to represent a typical usage period for the average consumer. The reference months for the first and second Reports were March 2011 and April 2012, respectively. The collection period for subsequent annual Reports was shifted to September[1] to standardize on an annual baseline reporting month. The reference month for this Report is September 2013, twelve months after the previous testing period. We will attempt to maintain this as our reporting month for future Reports when practical.

The methodologies and assumptions underlying the measurements described in this Report are reviewed at meetings that are open to all interested parties, and a public record of these meetings is maintained by the FCC. The techniques used as part of this study to gather data, and the data generated thereby, have the specific aim of profiling broadband Internet access services. That is, they are aimed at highlighting averages and trends in service characteristics within the scope of control of individual service providers.[2] The resulting view necessarily focuses only on the network properties being measured.

In this Report, we are pleased to again include results on satellite technology, based on test results collected from ViaSat/Exede, a major satellite services provider.[3] In our February 2013 Report we highlighted significant changes in satellite performance resulting from the satellite industry launching a new generation of satellites, beginning in 2011 with ViaSat's launch of their first Ka[4] band satellite, offering performance as much as 100 times[5] superior to previous generations. We include comparisons between satellite and wireline technologies in this Report and look forward to expanding the number of participating satellite providers in future Reports.

This Report, like the Reports that preceded it, could not have been produced without the counsel of a broad array of individuals and entities, collectively and informally referred to as "the broadband collaborative", which includes the participating ISPs, equipment manufacturers, M-Lab,[6] Level 3 Communications, and academics. Participation in this group is open and voluntary.

PRODUCTION OF THE REPORT

As with previous Reports, this Report relied on measurement hardware and software deployed in the homes of thousands of volunteer consumers. Although the "Whitebox" devices and software conduct automated, direct measurements of broadband performance throughout the year,[7] all testing represented in this Report was conducted in September 2013.[8] The Report focuses on four ISP delivery technologies—DSL, cable, fiber, and satellite – and examines offerings from 14 of the largest broadband providers,[9] which collectively account for well over 80 percent of U.S. residential broadband connections. The Technical Appendix for the Report provides specific information regarding the process by which these measurements were made and describes each test that was performed. The structure of this Report and the measurements represented herein largely track the February 2013 Report, which provides a useful baseline for comparison.

These Reports focus on performance during peak usage period, which is defined as weeknights between 7:00 pm to 11:00 pm local time. Focusing on peak usage period provides the most useful information because it demonstrates the kind of performance users can expect when the delivery of Internet service is under highest demand.

Throughout this Report, we use the term "advertised speed" to refer to the speed ISPs use in marketing their broadband service. We also use the term "sustained speed," which is speed averaged over a period of several seconds.[10] On a short time scale, broadband speeds may vary widely, at times approaching or even exceeding advertised speeds and at other times— due to network congestion—slowing to rates that may be well below advertised speeds. The "sustained speed" metric is designed to describe long-term average broadband performance.

It is important to note some limitations on the results contained in this Report. Generally, only the most popular service tiers among an ISP's offerings were tested, even though some service providers may offer other tiers not represented by volunteers contributing data to the program.[11] In addition, the data are analyzed at the national level, and are not collected in a way that permits meaningful conclusions about broadband performance at the local level.[12]

The basic objective of the Measuring Broadband America program is to measure broadband service performance as delivered by an ISP to the consumer. Although many factors contribute to end-to-end consumer broadband performance, this Report focuses on those elements under the direct or indirect control of a consumer's ISP, from the consumer gateway—the modem or router used by the consumer to access the Internet—to a nearby major Internet gateway point. Thus, any bandwidth limitations or delays incurred in the consumer's home, or in segments of the Internet outside an ISP's network, are not reflected in the results. Similarly, the results do not attempt to capture variations in how well an ISP is interconnected with Internet transit or content distribution network (CDN) providers. This focus aligns with key attributes of broadband service that are advertised to consumers, and allows a direct comparison across broadband providers of actual performance delivered to the household.

This program has given rise to benefits beyond the publication of this and previous Reports. We have worked with participants of this program to jointly propose broadband performance measurement standards will benefit consumers.[13] In addition, metrics based upon the work of this program are being incorporated into other programs of the Commission.[14] We are encouraged that many stakeholders have found this ongoing measurement study valuable, and that certain ISPs have adopted our methodology, developed their own internal broadband performance testing programs, and made improvements to their ongoing disclosures to consumers.

CHANGES TO TEST METHODOLOGY

Expansion of Testing Network

The Commission reached agreement with Level 3 Communications to include elements of its research network into the test architecture employed by the Commission for purposes of this study. Level 3 Communications is a major provider of IP-based services to other ISPs and businesses. The Commission began integrating Level 3 resources into its testing architecture in 2012[15]. After extensive testing, we have confidence in utilizing those resources as part of our testing process, and this is the first Report based on test results from both M-Lab and Level 3 Communications resources.[16] These additional resources increase the measurement network's resilience to localized degradation, and give us more flexibility in dealing with network faults which can hinder our test program. With this Report, we include measurements using the Level 3 Communications network in our reported results. A white paper describing the features of the Level 3 Communications research network is incorporated in the 2014 Technical Appendix.

Test Infrastructure and Measurement Calibration

Prior to initiating data collection for use in our Reports, we perform a variety of comparative tests across the multiple test servers in our data collection network to ensure that the testing infrastructure that supports the collection of test results is performing optimally. During preparation for the data collection for this Report, we identified a performance issue associated with elements in our measurement network connected to some of the ISPs under study. Discussions with participants in open meetings suggested that network degradations were likely on the inter-domain path between these measurement servers and the ISPs to be measured.

Further, it was widely reported in the press that business disputes between some of the participating providers and Cogent Communications (Cogent), a company providing connectivity between some measurement servers and the providers, were resulting in congestion at interconnection points and network paths between the parties.[17] Since our test traffic is carried over these same interconnecting paths, this congestion would also affect our tests. Regardless of the cause, these performance degradations presented several challenges for our study.

First, our existing policy is to exclude measurements from our Report known to have been collected from a degraded measurements infrastructure affecting our testing. Our prior experience had been that such degradations were the result of network faults which were soon corrected and outside the scope of an ISP's control. Second, we attempt to provide a perspective on the average performance across an access provider's network which can consist of thousands of interconnecting paths. Our testing in this case had demonstrated that only certain paths were impacted, not all paths.

Based on our examination of the issue and its path specific nature, the impact of this degradation on any given consumer's performance is variable, and will differ for some customers as compared to others. The majority of consumers accessing services through the many interconnection points within a service provider's network would likely not be severely impacted by this situation. We also recognize, however, that those consumers accessing services and content over the affected paths would likely see a significant degradation in their service. As our Report focuses on average network performance and based on our analysis of this situation, we have chosen to rely upon data from unaffected servers for results in this Report. This decision is consistent with our existing policies. We have also collected test results from impacted servers and are releasing this data as part of our reporting process for use by academics and others in examination of this issue. We are continuing to gather data related to this issue and will make adjustments to our policy as necessary in the future to continue to provide reliable data on ISP performance.

Legacy Modems

In previous Reports, we discussed the challenges ISPs face in improving network performance where equipment under the control of the subscriber limits the end-to-end performance achievable by the subscriber.[18] In this Report, we review the capabilities of cable modems within the homes of consumer volunteers participating in this study. This information is important because measured end-to-end service performance of cable broadband service is a function both of the capabilities of the service provider's network and of the capabilities of the cable modem which terminates the service within a subscriber's home. In other words, a consumer's ability to actually receive the provider's advertised speeds depends upon the capabilities of the cable modems within their home.

Cable ISPs have described two scenarios where these issues may affect the results of this study. First, some consumers own their modems and have not yet upgraded to take advantage of the higher speeds enabled by DOCSIS 3, the latest standard cable technology. Second, some consumers who lease cable modems and have been provided with free upgrades nonetheless may have failed to install these new modems at the time of data collection. Cable ISPs requested that we review our sample of volunteers and identify panelists using legacy equipment that would not achieve the provisioned capacity available to the consumer and thus would introduce a possible inaccuracy in measured performance of the network under actual control of the ISP.

In response, we developed a proposal that included several conditions on participating ISPs. First, proposed changes in consumer panelists would only be considered where an ISP was offering free upgrades for modems they owned and leased to the consumer. Second, each ISP needed to disclose its policy regarding the treatment of legacy modems and its efforts to inform consumers regarding the impact such modems may have on their service. (These statements are included as an appendix to this Report.) Finally, we would continue to collect data from our existing panelists, and report on aggregated results across all ISPs by technology. These charts would help assess any changes resulting from this policy change and help quantify the overall impact of legacy modems on consumer performance.

These issues were discussed in open meetings among a range of participants. Participants generally were supportive of our proposal. We also noted that while the issue of DOCSIS 3 modems and network upgrades affect the cable industry today, this is a general issue concerning network investment and evolution and the impact on equipment that the provider places within the consumer's household and is under their direct control.

Consistent with our proposal, this Report includes data collected from additional panelists using modems compatible with the provisioned speed tier. Panelists with non-conforming modems are not included in ISPs' reported results, but are tracked separately in charts displaying any difference between the two sets of panelists.

We further note that, based on the analysis of data collected for this Report and information made available by service providers, the Commission believes that the issues associated with the use of legacy equipment likely would affect subscribers with services tiers of 15Mbps or higher. And for subscribers in tiers above 20 Mbps, any effects will likely be more pronounced. In particular, as reflected in the following charts, the impact of this proposed change appears to be slight at this time. However, as ISPs evolve to higher and higher speeds, we believe this might change. As such, we will continue to track this metric.

We also note that these charts depict the impact on the overall market of legacy modems and not the impact on a specific consumer which may be greater than the aggregate impact. We will continue to monitor this issue as network speeds continue to evolve. We are now at a tipping point for broadband technology where available network speeds are beginning to challenge the capabilities of the consumer's home broadband environment. For those consumers moving to speed tiers of 15 Mbps or higher, the impact of a legacy modem can be extremely significant.

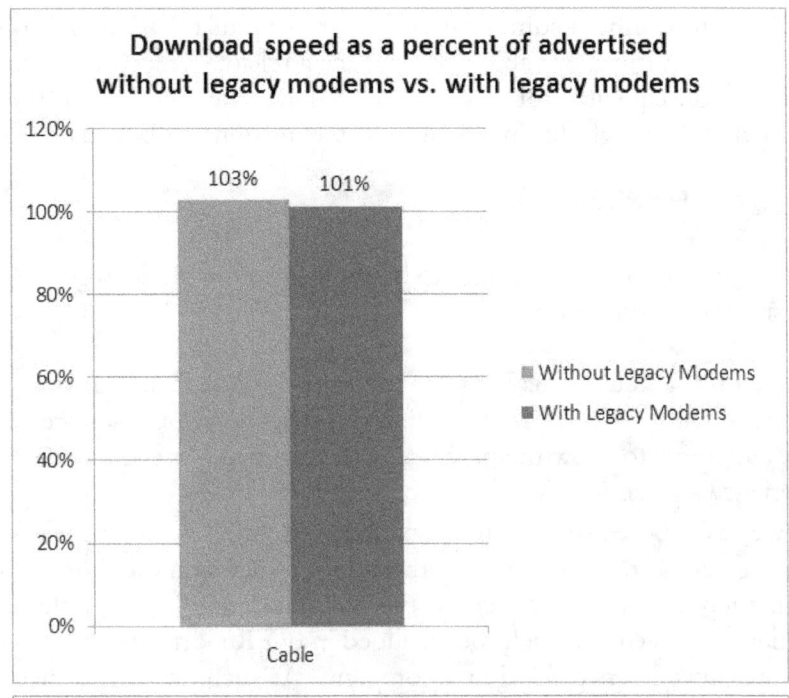

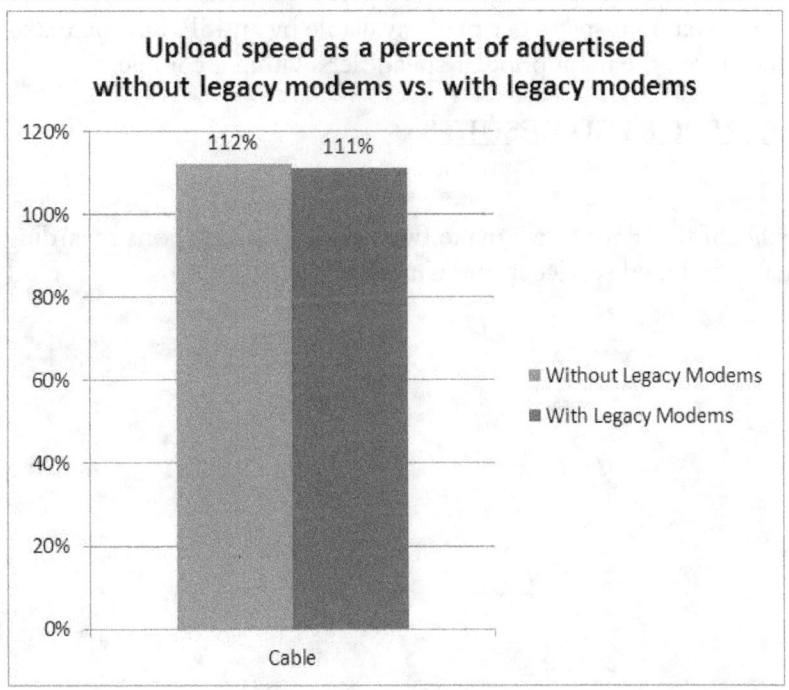

ViaSat/Exede Data Consumption

In our last Report, we included charts describing customers' data consumption (i.e., bytes downloaded or uploaded per month) for each ISP in our study. Our ability to calculate this metric depends upon how the Whitebox is installed and configured in the household. As our program has evolved, we have moved to a Whitebox configuration which has eased consumer installation, but this is not without some drawbacks. In particular, ViaSat has noted that this newer configuration complicates our ability to produce a reliable data consumption metric for satellite broadband. Consequently, for this Report, we have removed ViaSat/Exede from the data consumption charts, though this information is included in our bulk data releases.

NEW METRICS & CHARTS

In this Report, we introduce two new charts to better inform the public regarding overall performance of surveyed service providers.

- First, based on suggestions made by the Institute for Advanced Analytics - North Carolina State University, we are introducing a chart describing service consistency[19]. This chart attempts to show the percentage of time that a specific percentage of users will experience a given (or higher) service speed.
- Second, we have started to track the maximum upload/download speeds offered by an ISP in a given year. Our survey methodology focuses on the most popular service tiers for the reported years. Generally, this will translate to an ISP's three to six most popular tiers. A speed tier might be excluded in our Report if it was not among the most popular speed tiers offered by a company. As such, we are not necessarily tracking the maximum speed tier made available by an ISP, but the maximum speed as reported across the most popular speed tiers within a company.

OVERVIEW OF REPORTED RESULTS

Based on the results of this Report, we make five primary observations regarding the current state of residential broadband service in the United States.

1. Many ISPs now closely meet or exceed the speeds they advertise, but there continues to be room for improvement.

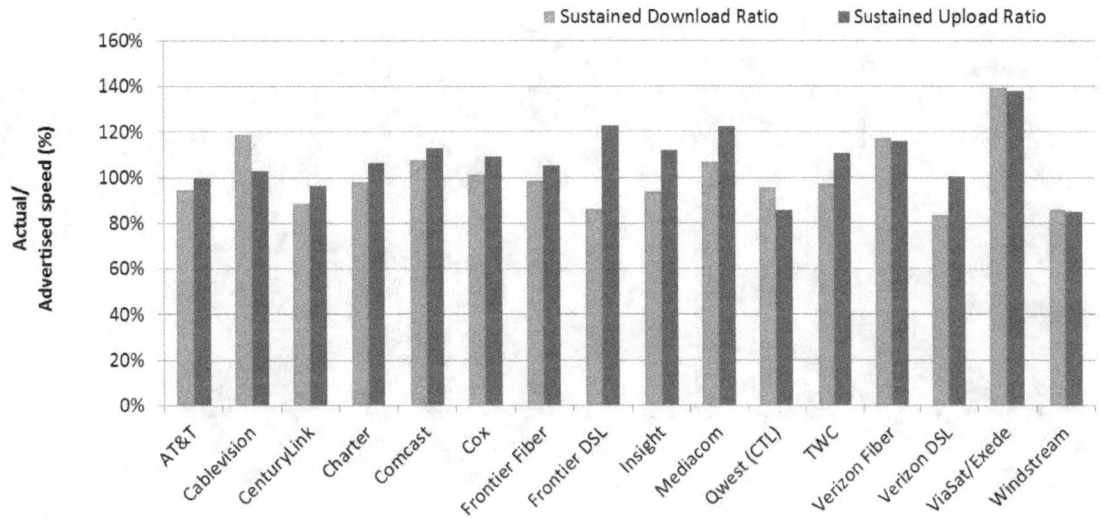

This chart compares upload and download performance during peak usage periods across all ISPs. All ISPs, except for Verizon DSL, CenturyLink, Frontier DSL and Windstream, meet 90 percent of performance or better, on average, during peak periods. Notably, these four ISPs use DSL technology.

2. New metric this year – Consistency of speeds – also shows significant room for improvement.

Implementing a suggestion made by researchers at North Carolina State University, this latest report includes a metric designed to convey how likely any given consumer is to experience broadband speeds of a particular level. Cablevision, for example, delivered 100 percent or better of advertised speed to 80 percent of our panelists 80 percent of the time during peak periods, and about half the ISPs delivered less than about 90 percent or better of the advertised speed for 80/80. However about one-third of the ISPs delivered only 60 percent or better of advertised speeds 80 percent of the time to 80 percent of the consumers. This is a metric that we expect ISPs to improve upon over the course of the next year.

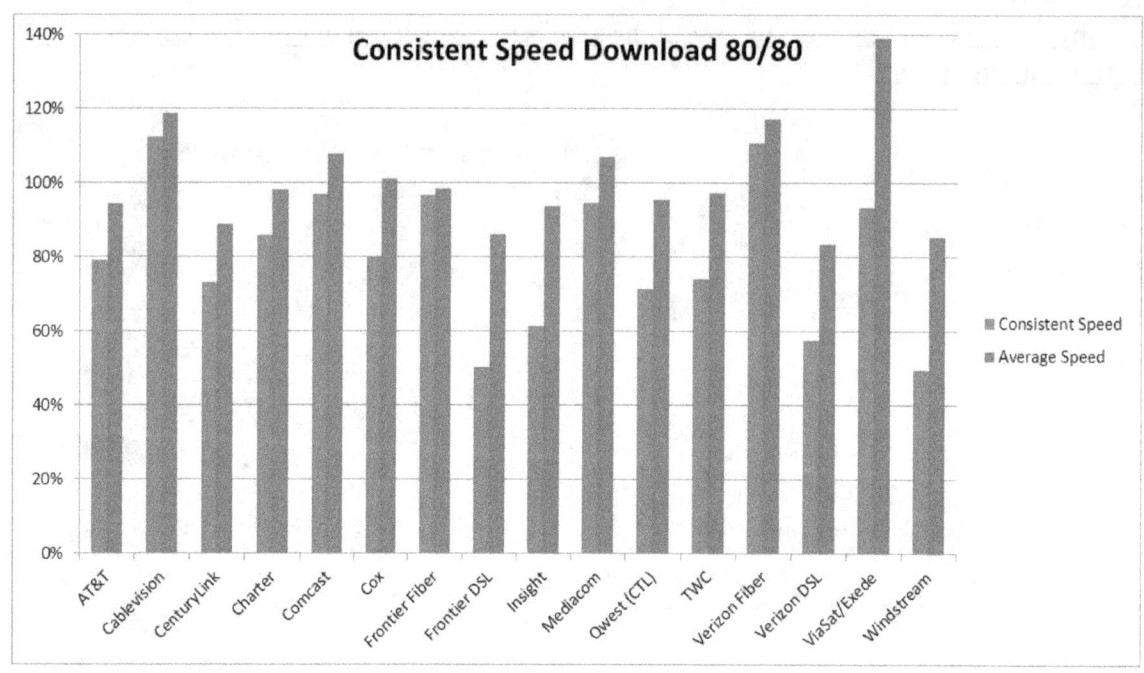

3. Consumers are continuing to migrate to faster speed tiers.

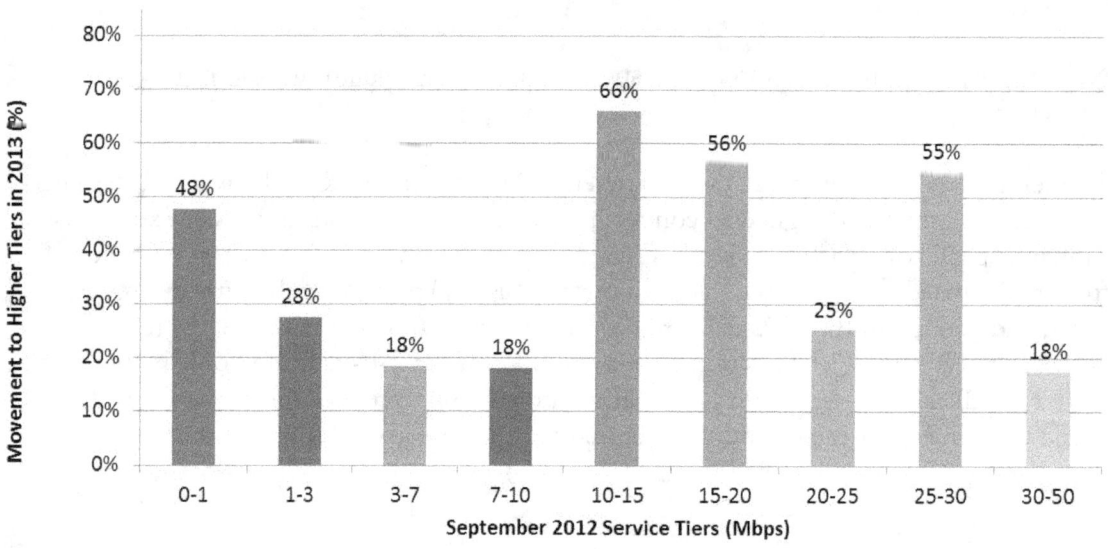

This chart shows that consumers are moving to faster speed tiers, continuing the trend that we highlighted both in the February 2013 Report and the July 2012 Report. Specifically, the bars represent the percentage of volunteers from each of the September 2012 tested speed tiers that moved to a higher speed tier by the September 2013 testing period. Movement to a higher speed tier can occur in two ways: 1) a consumer can subscribe to a higher tier from the same or competing ISP or 2) an ISP can upgrade service for all consumers within a specific service tier. In our tests of download speed, we added five new tiers above 30 Mbps from the last testing period,[20] and our tests of upload performance included one additional offering above 8 Mbps.[21] In this Report, we find the average subscribed speed is now 21.2 Mbps, representing an average annualized speed increase of about 36 percent from the 15.6 Mbps average of 2012.

4. Improvements in Speed are not Uniform Across Speed Tiers Tested

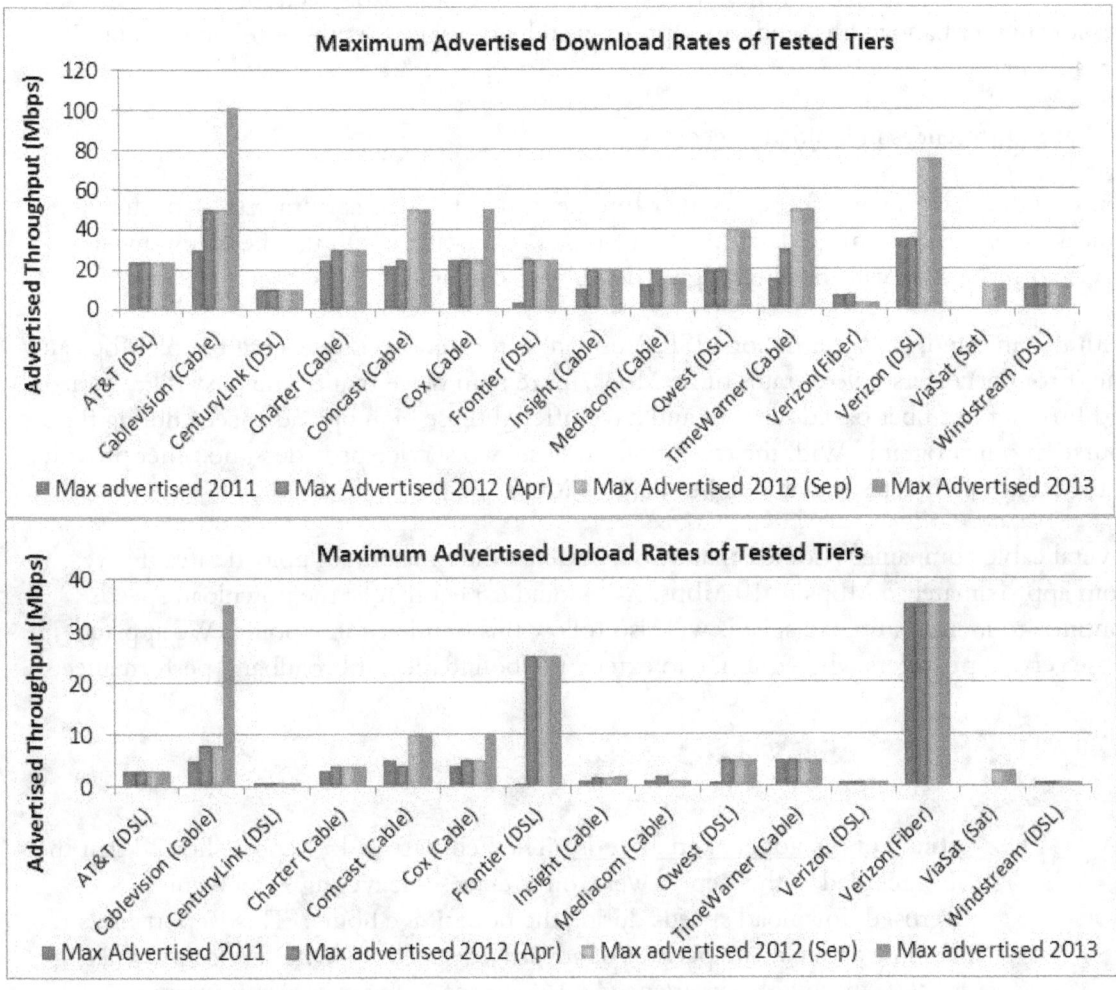

Our report focuses on the most popular speed tiers offered by an ISP- that is, the maximum speed used by a major percentage of an ISPs consumers. We note that a particular ISP may offer faster speed tiers either throughout their territory or in specific portions of their territory that are not as popular as the speed tiers we tested. However, as the Commission's goal is to advance high speed Internet access to all Americans, we believe highlighting the maximum speed *among the popular speed tiers*, is the most effective way to demonstrate the spread of high speed Internet access.

While the average increase in network speed tier was about 36 percent, the results are not uniform over ISP and technology types. Most notably, those ISPs using DSL technology show little or no improvement in maximum speeds, with the sole exception of Qwest/Centurylink, which this past year doubled its highest download speed within specific market areas. The reason for this may be that DSL, unlike cable and fiber technologies, is strongly dependent upon the length of the copper wire (or "loop") from the residence to the service provider's terminating electronic equipment, such that obtaining higher data speeds would require companies to make significant capital investments across a market area to shorten the copper loops. On the other hand, both fiber and cable technologies intrinsically support higher bandwidths, and can support even higher speeds with more incremental investments.

5. Sharp Differences in Upload Speeds

Many studies have shown that consumer Internet traffic today is asymmetric – consumers typically download far more data than they upload. Consistent with that behavior, most service offerings typically have far higher download than upload rates.

With this in mind, we note that one ISP (Verizon) offers upload rates as high as 35 Mbps and one (Frontier) offers upload rates of 25 Mbps, more than twice that of the next ISP. Verizon and Frontier use fiber based services and have offered these high upload speeds during the course of our program. With the exception of these two service providers, no other provider in the study offers rates that are higher than 10 Mbps.

Several cable companies (Comcast and Cox) doubled their maximum upload rates this year from approximately 5 Mbps to 10 Mbps. We would expect that as the download speeds continue to increase, upload speeds will also follow this trend at some point. We applaud those service providers who continue to extend the boundaries of broadband performance.

Major Findings of the Study

- **Actual versus advertised speeds.** The February 2013 Report showed that the ISPs included in the Report were, on average,[22] delivering 97 percent of advertised download speeds during the peak usage hours. This Report finds that ISPs now provide 101 percent of advertised speeds.[23] One service provider, Qwest/Centurylink, experienced a 16 percent performance improvement.

- **Sustained download speeds as a percentage of advertised speeds.** The average actual sustained download speed during peak periods was calculated as a percentage of the ISP's advertised speed. This calculation was done for each speed tier offered by each ISP.

  o *Results by technology:*

- On average, during peak periods DSL-based services delivered download speeds that were 91 percent of advertised speeds, cable-based services delivered 102 percent of advertised speeds, fiber-to-the-home services delivered 113 percent of advertised speeds, and satellite delivered 138 percent of advertised speeds. These results suggest that many ISPs are meeting established engineering goals for their respective technologies.

- Peak period speeds decreased from 24-hour average speeds[24] by 2.7 percent for fiber-to-the-home services, 3.8 percent for DSL-based services, 4.2 percent for cable-based services and 6.8 percent for satellite services. The differences are largely in line with results observed in the February 2013 Report, though the 6.8 percent decrease in peak over 24 hour performance for satellite services was an increase over the 4.4 percent change in performance observed for satellite service in 2013.

   o *Results by ISP*:

      - Average peak period download speeds per ISP varied from a high of 139 percent of advertised speed (ViaSat/Exede) to a low of 83 percent of advertised speed (Verizon DSL). These results are largely consistent with the February 2013 Reports[25].

      - In this Report, there was a 3.9 percent decrease in performance between 24 hour and peak averages.[26] This would be consistent with higher demands on network usage across consumer participants.

- **Sustained upload speeds as a percentage of advertised speeds.** On average, across all ISPs, upload speed was 107 percent of advertised speed, closely matching results in last year's February 2013 Report of 108 percent.[27] Across almost all carriers, upload speeds showed little evidence of congestion with small variance between 24 hour averages and peak period averages[28]. The sole exception was satellite, which showed a 5 percent drop in performance from 24 hour average to peak period, though it still remained above 100 percent.

   o *Results by technology*: On average, satellite services delivered 138 percent, fiber-to-the-home 114 and cable-based services delivered 111 percent, and DSL-based services delivered 98 percent of advertised upload speeds.

   o *Results by ISP*: Average upload speeds among ISPs ranged from a low of 85 percent of advertised speed to a high of 138 percent of advertised speed.

- **Latency.** Latency is the time it takes for a data packet to travel from one point to another in a network, and is commonly expressed in terms of milliseconds (ms). Latency can be a major factor in overall performance of Internet services. Latency can be expressed as a one-way or round-trip time. In all our tests and results, latency is defined as the round-trip time from the consumer's home to the closest speed measurement server within the provider's network and back.[29]

o Across all terrestrial technologies during peak periods, latency averaged 34. 9 ms. This is an increase over the February 2013 Report figure of 29.6 ms.[30] (This increase in latency is likely at least partly the result of the changes in using test servers discussed earlier. By excluding certain servers whose paths were found to be congested, we would invariably be forcing some traffic over longer paths to alternate servers, increasing latency.) Satellite systems involve the transmission of information over long distances and have correspondingly higher latencies than for terrestrial technologies. ViaSat had a measured latency of 671.1 ms, approximately 19 times the terrestrial average.

o During peak periods, latency increased across all terrestrial technologies by between 12% and 19%.[31] In last year's Report, this figure was 10 percent. Since the transmission distances involved dominate satellite latency, it shows no perceptible (less than 1 percent) variance between peak and 24 hour periods.

- *Results by technology:*

  - Latency was lowest in fiber-to-the-home services.

  - Fiber-to-the-home services provided 24 ms round-trip latency on average, while cable-based services averaged 32 ms, and DSL-based services averaged 49 ms.

- *Results by ISP:* The highest average round-trip latency for an individual terrestrial service tier, i.e. excluding satellite, was 57.91 ms (Qwest/Centurylink), while the lowest average latency within a single service tier was 17.83 ms (Cablevision).

- **Effect of burst speed techniques.** As discussed in prior Reports, some cable operators offer burst speed techniques, marketed under names such as "PowerBoost," which temporarily allocate more bandwidth to a consumer's service. The effect is temporary—it typically lasts less than 15 to 20 seconds— and may be reduced by other broadband activities occurring within the consumer household.[32] Burst speed is not equivalent to sustained speed. Sustained speed is a better measure of how well certain activities may be supported by a particular service. For example, large file transfers, video streaming, and video chat, require the transfer of large amounts of information over sustained periods of time. However, other activities – such as web browsing or gaming – often require the transfer of moderate amounts of information in a short interval of time. Such services may benefit from burst speed techniques, though the actual effect depends on a number of factors.

- o Burst speed techniques increased short-term download performance by as much as 29.3 percent over sustained speeds during peak periods for Mediacom, and by more than 10 percent for five other providers. The benefits of burst techniques are most evident at intermediate speeds of around 8 to 15 Mbps and appear to tail off at much higher speeds.

- **Web Browsing, Voice over Internet Protocol (VoIP), and Streaming Video.**

  - o *Web browsing.* In specific tests designed to mimic basic web browsing—accessing a series of web pages, but not streaming video or using video chat sites or applications—the total time needed to load a page decreased with higher speeds. However, the performance increase diminishes beyond about 10 Mbps, as latency and other factors begin to dominate. For these high speed tiers, consumers are unlikely to experience much if any improvement in basic web browsing from increased speed–*i.e.*, moving from a 10 Mbps broadband offering to a 25 Mbps offering. To be sure, this is from the perspective of a single user employing a web browser. Higher speeds may provide significant advantages in a multi-user household, or where a consumer is using a specific application that may be able to benefit from a higher speed tier.

  - o *VoIP.* VoIP services were adequately supported by all of the service tiers discussed in this Report.[33] However, VoIP quality may suffer during times when household bandwidth is shared by other services. The VoIP measurements utilized for this Report were not designed to detect such effects.

  - o *Streaming Video.* The results published in this Report suggest that video streaming will work across all technologies tested, though the quality of the video that can be streamed will depend upon the speed. For example, standard definition video is currently commonly transmitted at speeds from 1 Mbps to 2 Mbps. High quality video can demand faster speeds, with full HD (1080p) demanding 5 Mbps[34] or more for a single stream. Consumers should understand the requirements of the streaming video they want to use and ensure that their chosen broadband service tier will meet those requirements, including when multiple members of a household simultaneously want to watch streaming video on separate devices.[35]

- **Variability of Performance.** In the last Report, we added a new category of charts to track variability of performance of a service provider. We provide that data again, in this Report. We have calculated the percentage of users across a range of advertised speeds that experience, on average, performance levels at that speed or better. This information, commonly called a cumulative distribution function, shows how speed is distributed across the population of consumers included in this survey. As in the previous Report, the results reported herein demonstrate that consumers should be reasonably confident that the performance they receive from their ISP will be consistent with the results reflected in this Report. Also, as discussed earlier, in this Report we have expanded our measurements on variability by including charts suggested by the Institute of Advanced Analytics emphasizing the consistency of services delivered to consumers.

- **Satellite Broadband.** In this Report we include results for ViaSat, a satellite-based broadband service provider. Satellite-based broadband Internet services differ from terrestrial-based services in several key ways. First, because satellites broadcast wirelessly directly to the consumer, no actual terrestrial infrastructure has to be deployed. As a result, satellite technologies have a more uniform cost structure, which is unique among the technologies under study in our Report.

Satellite facilities have historically had impairments which have limited their competitiveness with other broadband services. For example, limited bandwidth reduced the service speeds that could be offered to consumers. In addition, latency has been an order of magnitude greater than with terrestrial broadband technologies. Communicating with a geosynchronous satellite orbiting the earth at a distance of greater than 36,000 km results in a round trip latency of about 500 ms.[36] The necessary signaling between the set-top box and the satellite controller, to request assignment of a communication channel, can double this to over 1000 ms, which would precluded use of many latency-sensitive services. In contrast, the maximum average latency found in our surveys for terrestrial technologies is less than 70 ms.

These differences in technology, including the effects that latency can have on some services,[37] make direct comparisons between satellite services and terrestrial-based broadband services difficult. Nevertheless, beginning in 2011, the consumer broadband satellite industry began launching a new generation of satellites designed to improve overall performance significantly. The launch of a new generation of Ka band satellites represents an important advance in consumer based satellite service which will benefit those consumers under-served by terrestrial alternatives. For example, in October of 2011, ViaSat launched its ViaSat-1 satellite, which has an overall capacity of 140 Gb/s.[38] In addition, ViaSat and other satellite industry operators have reduced overall latency by making improvements to other elements of their architecture.

Differences in service offerings compound the difficulty of direct comparisons between satellite and terrestrial offerings. Terrestrial-based service providers typically price by service speed, with some ISPs imposing data caps or some other form of consumption-based pricing. In contrast, ViaSat offers a single service speed, but provides service tiers in the form of different data caps: 10 gigabytes (GB), 15 GB, or 25 GB per month,[39] with unmetered downloads permitted between midnight and 5:00 a.m. local time.

Online Resources

In conjunction with this study, the Commission will make the following resources available to the public and research community.[40] The Commission is releasing this material in the hope that independent study of this data set will provide additional insights into consumer broadband services.

- **2014 Fixed Report**: http://data.fcc.gov/download/measuring-broadband-america/2014/2014-Fixed-Measuring-Broadband-America-Report.pdf

- **2014 Fixed Report Technical Appendix**: http://data.fcc.gov/download/measuring-broadband-america/2014/Technical-Appendix-fixed-2014.pdf

- **Charts in 2014 Fixed Report**: http://www.fcc.gov/measuring-broadband-america/2014/charts-fixed-2014

- **Validated Data Set**: (for charts in 2014 Report): http://www.fcc.gov/measuring-broadband-america/2014/validated-data-fixed-2014

- **Methodology Resources**: (how data is collected and calculated): http://www.fcc.gov/measuring-broadband-america/2014/methodology-fixed-report-2014

- **Tabular Test Results**: (data sets recorded during the September 2013 testing period): http://www.fcc.gov/measuring-broadband-america/2014/tabular-test-results-fixed-2014

- **Raw Bulk Data Set:** (complete, non-validated results for all tests run during the September 2013 testing period): http://www.fcc.gov/measuring-broadband-america/2014/raw-data-fixed-2013

- **February 2013 Report, Technical Appendix, and Data Sets:** http://www.fcc.gov/measuring-broadband-america/2013/February

- **July 2012 Report, Technical Appendix, and Data Sets:** http://www.fcc.gov/measuring-broadband-america/2012/july

- **August 2011 Report, Technical Appendix, and Data Sets:** http://www.fcc.gov/measuring-broadband-america/2011/august

Description of Tests

The information reflected in this Report is based on 13 separate measurements that can be used to characterize various aspects of broadband performance to the consumer. Participants agreed to base the Report on one month's worth of data, and to use September 2013 as the test month. September 2013 data were verified and are analyzed in this Report. Active data collection continued after September, and while this subsequent data set has not been verified or analyzed, it is included in the Raw Bulk Data Set that will be released to the public.[41]

As in previous Reports, this Report emphasizes two metrics that are of particular relevance to consumers: speed and latency. Broadband throughput or speed is the primary performance characteristic advertised by ISPs. Broadband speed is the average rate at which information "packets" are delivered successfully over the communications channel. A higher speed indicates a higher information delivery rate. For example, a 10 Mbps service should deliver ten times as much information as a 1 Mbps service in a given period of time.[42]

The use of transient performance enhancements, such as burst speed techniques, present a technical challenge when measuring speed. Services featuring such enhancements will deliver a far higher throughput for short periods. For example, a user who has purchased a 6 Mbps service tier might receive 18 Mbps for the first 10 megabytes (MB) of a particular download. This is of significant benefit to applications such as web browsing, which use relatively short-lived connections to transfer short bursts of data. But once the burst window lapses, throughput will return to the base rate, making the burst rate an inaccurate measure of performance for longer, sustained data transfers. In addition, other household broadband activities may reduce or even eliminate the benefit of the speed burst. The tests employed in this study isolated the effects of transient performance-enhancing features, and the Report presents sustained and "burst" speed results separately, as both metrics could be relevant to users with different needs and usage patterns.

Latency is another key factor in broadband performance.[43] The impact of latency is felt in a number of ways. For example, high round-trip latency may compromise the quality of voice services in ways that are perceptible to consumers[44] and may interfere with playing interactive games[45]. Latency also affects the rate of information transmission for the transmission control protocol ("TCP"), which is commonly used to support Internet applications, and can therefore limit the maximum actual speed achievable for a broadband service. Some operations consist of a sequence of network tasks, and thus the effect of network latencies may add up. Thus, latency can have a significant effect on the performance of applications running across a computer network. As service speeds increase, the impact of network latency becomes more noticeable and has a more significant impact on overall performance.

One of the key factors affecting all aspects of broadband performance is the time of day. Specifically, at peak hours more people are attempting to use broadband connections, giving rise to a greater potential for congestion and degraded user performance.

This Report highlights the results of the following tests of broadband speed and latency, as measured on a national basis, across DSL, cable, fiber-to-the-home, and satellite technologies:

- **Sustained download speed**: throughput in Mbps utilizing three concurrent TCP connections measured at the 25-30 second interval of a sustained data transfer;

- **Sustained upload speed**: throughput in Mbps utilizing three concurrent TCP connections measured at the 25-30 second interval of a sustained data transfer;

- **Burst download speed**: throughput in Mbps utilizing three concurrent TCP connections measured at the 0-5 second interval of a sustained data transfer

- **Burst upload speed**: throughput in Mbps utilizing three concurrent TCP connections measured at the 0-5 second interval of a sustained data transfer

- **UDP latency**: average round trip time for a series of randomly transmitted user datagram protocol (UDP) packets distributed over a long timeframe

Overall, a total of 8 billion measurements were taken across 177 million unique tests.

Data derived from all tests performed is available on our website at http://www.fcc.gov/measuring-broadband-america.

Test Results

We present the summary of our findings below.[46] The Commission is separately releasing a Validated Data Set[47] on which this Report was based, and will also release a Raw Bulk Data Set of non-validated data collected outside the reference month. The results below are reported by performance variation, by ISP, and by technology (DSL, cable, fiber-to-the-home, and satellite) for the most popular service tiers offered by each ISP. As noted above, we focus on periods of consumption during peak periods. The results presented below represent average measured performance across a range of consumers, and while these results are useful for comparison purposes, they should not be taken as an indicator of performance for any specific consumer.

All charts below use data from September 2013 unless otherwise noted. We also include a chart comparing data from September 2013 and September 2012.

VARIATION BY ISP AND SERVICE TIER IN DELIVERY OF ADVERTISED SPEED

Chart 1 shows actual speed as a percentage of advertised speed both over a 24-hour period and during peak periods across all ISPs. In the September 2013 testing period, the majority of ISPs delivered actual download speeds during peak periods within 80 to 140 percent of advertised speeds or better, with modest performance declines during peak periods.[48]

Chart 1: Average Peak Period and 24-Hour Sustained Download Speeds as a Percentage of Advertised, by Provider—September 2013 Test Data

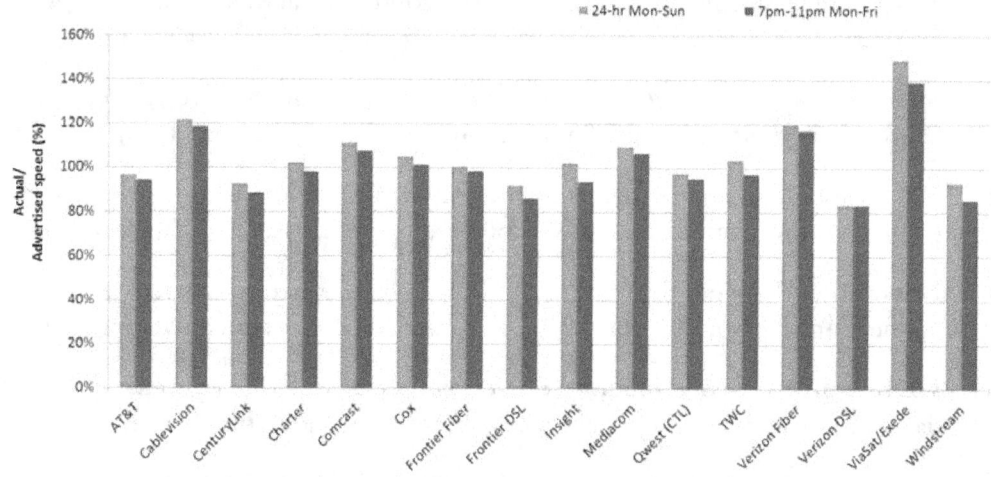

As shown in Chart 2, upload performance in the September 2013 test data is much less affected than download performance during peak periods. This is consistent with our findings in previous Reports.

Chart 2: Average Peak Period and 24-Hour Sustained Upload Speeds as a Percentage of Advertised, by Provider—September 2013 Test Data

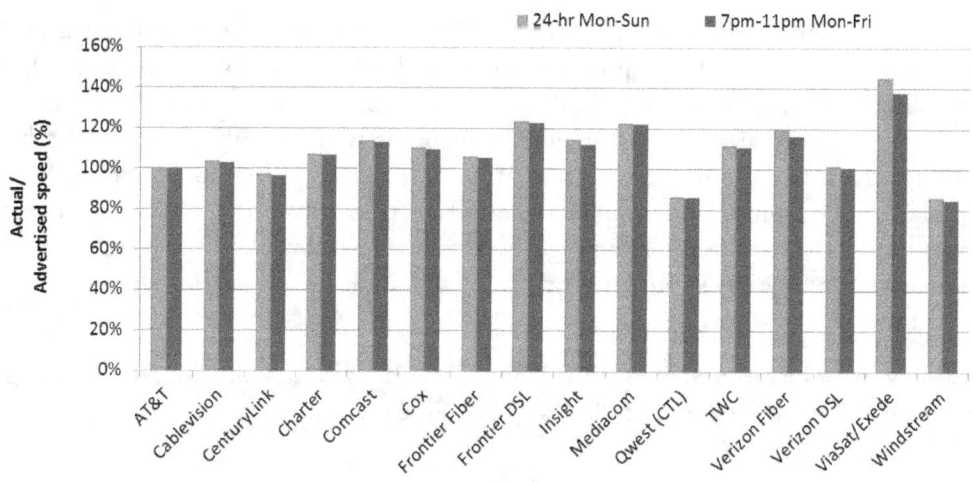

Chart 3 compares upload and download performance during peak periods across all ISPs.

Chart 3: Average Peak Period Sustained Download and Upload Speeds as a Percentage of Advertised, by Provider—September 2013 Test Data

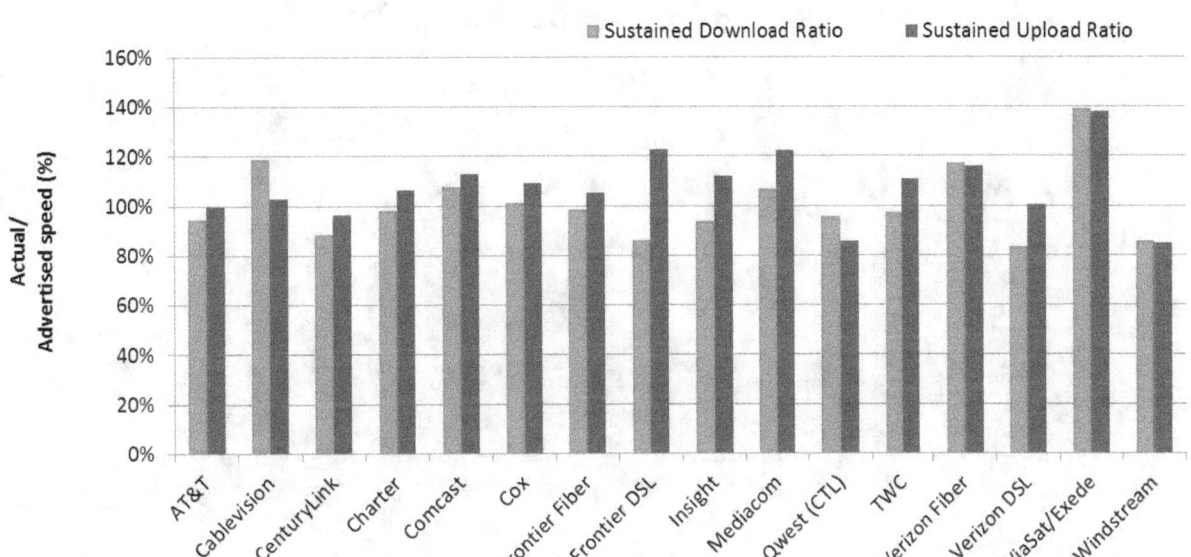

CONSISTENCY OF SPEEDS

Implementing a suggestion made by researchers at the Institute for Advanced Analytics – North Carolina State University, this Report includes information on the percent of users consistently receiving a specific level of broadband performance. To do this, the charts below show a specified percentage of users that receive an indicated percent of the advertised speed a specified percent of time. For example, for a specification of 70/70 (70 percent of people/70 percent of the time), consistent speed would indicate the minimum percent of advertised speed received by 70 percent of the consumers surveyed 70 percent of the time. In that chart, AT&T's consistent speed is 84 percent of advertised speed, indicating that 70 percent of our panelists received 84 percent or better of advertised speed 70 percent of the time. The metric shows what a given percentage of users receive, and may be helpful to consumers in understanding how consistently they may experience a particular level of performance. To be sure, the results are not a guarantee of a particular level of performance, though they do convey how likely any given consumer is to experience performance at the indicated level.

Chart 4: Percent of Advertised to Actual Download Performance of Seventy Percent of Panelists' Experience by Provider in September 2013

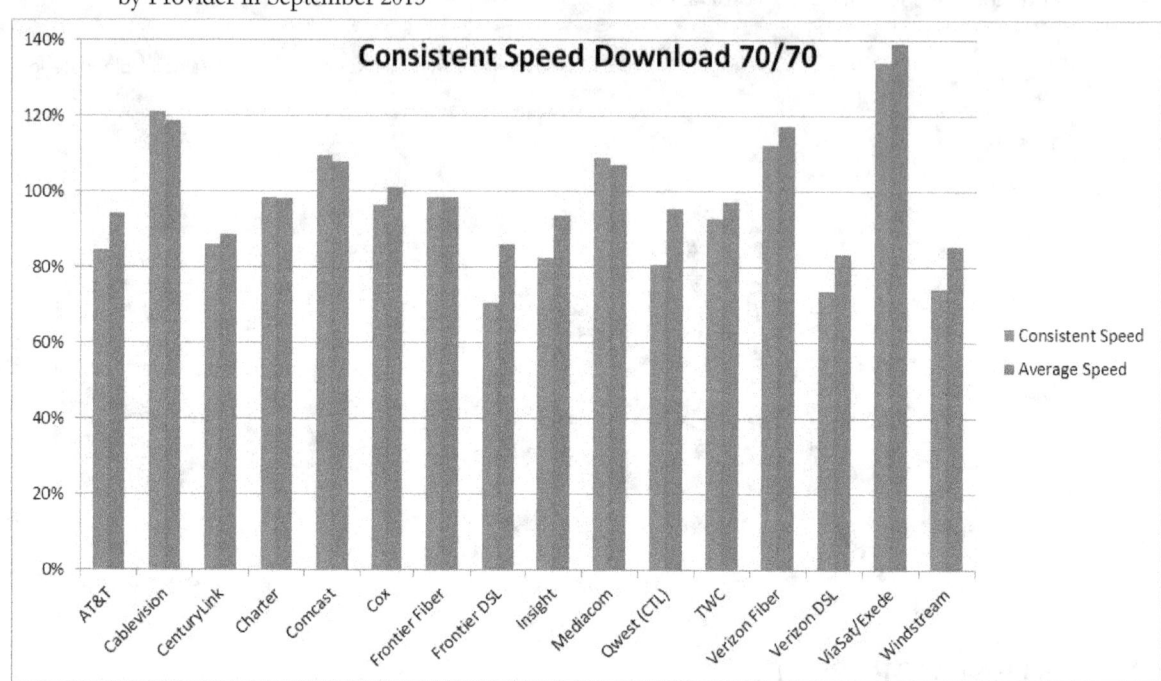

Chart 5: Percent of Advertised to Actual Upload Performance of Seventy Percent of Panelists' Experience by Provider in September 2013

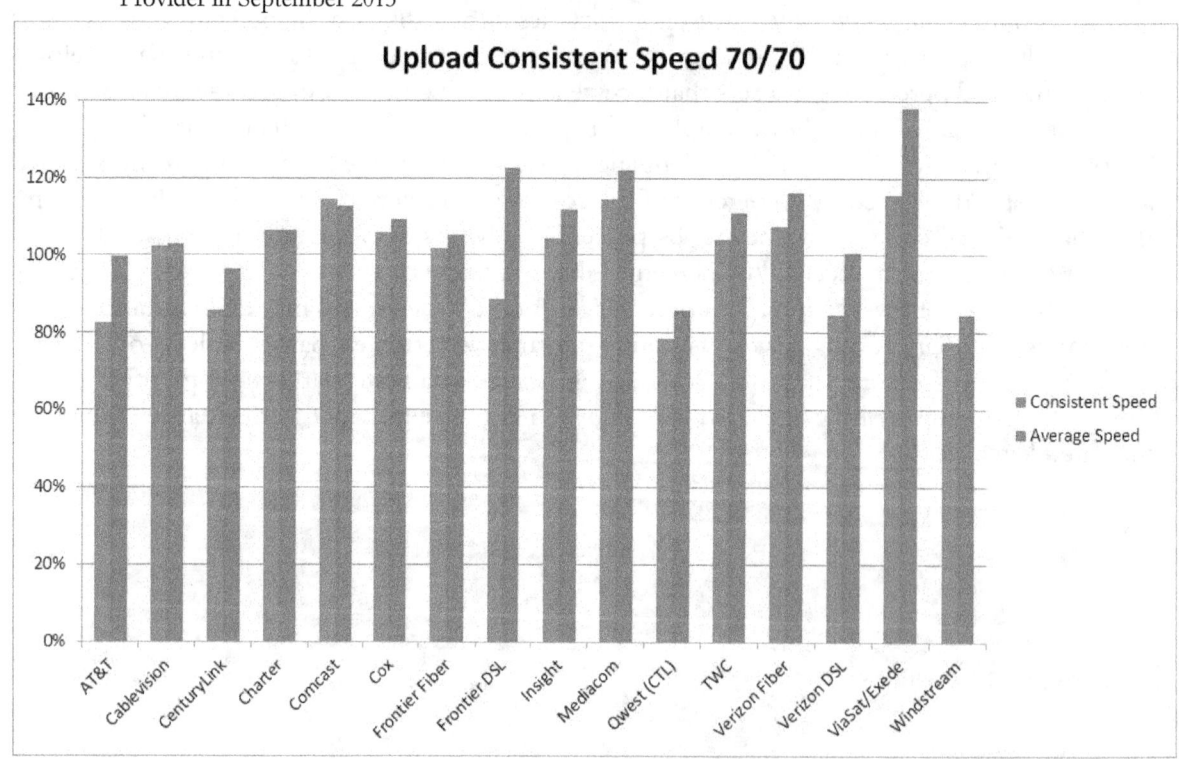

Chart 6: Percent of Advertised to Actual Download Performance of Eighty Percent of Panelists' Experience by Provider in September 2013

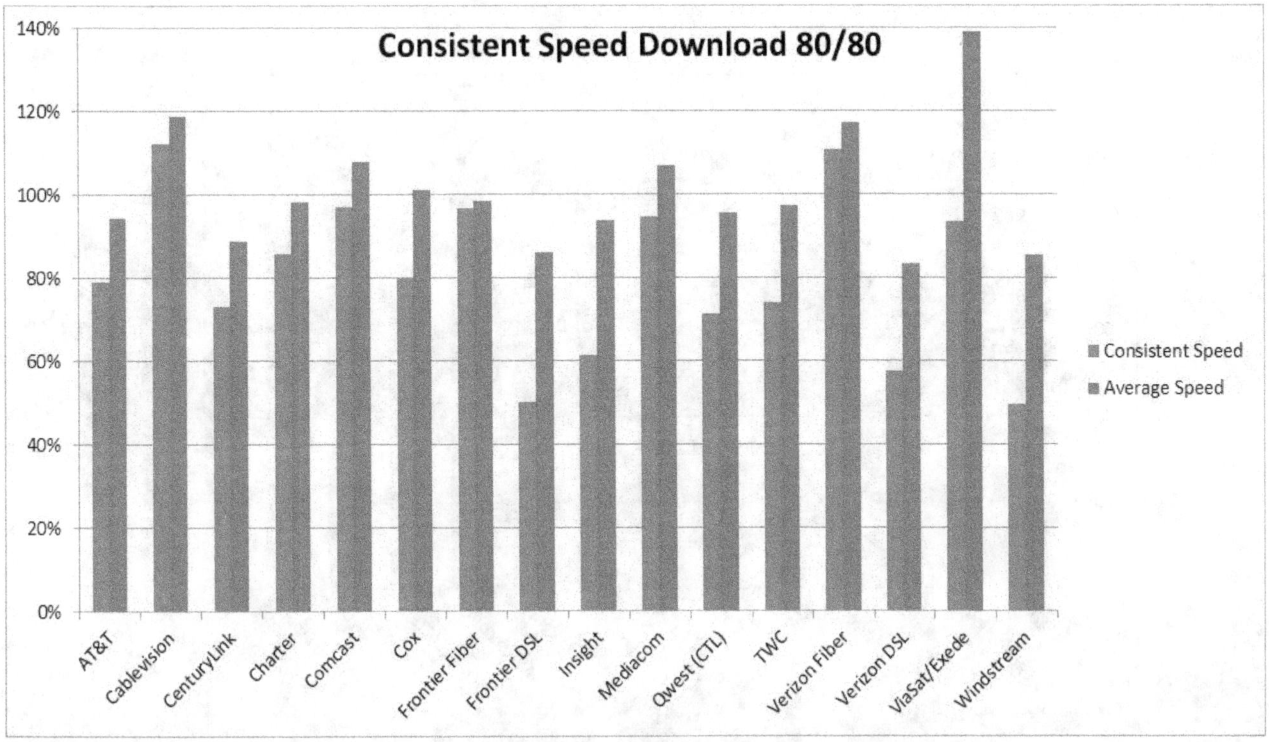

It can be seen from the above chart that, for example, 80 percent of Cablevision and Verizon Fiber customers receive over 100 percent of advertised download speeds 80 percent of the time. The "% Advertised" values are presented for comparison and reflect the values in Chart 3.

Chart 7: Percent of Advertised to Actual Upload Performance of Eighty Percent of Panelists' Experience by Provider in September 2013

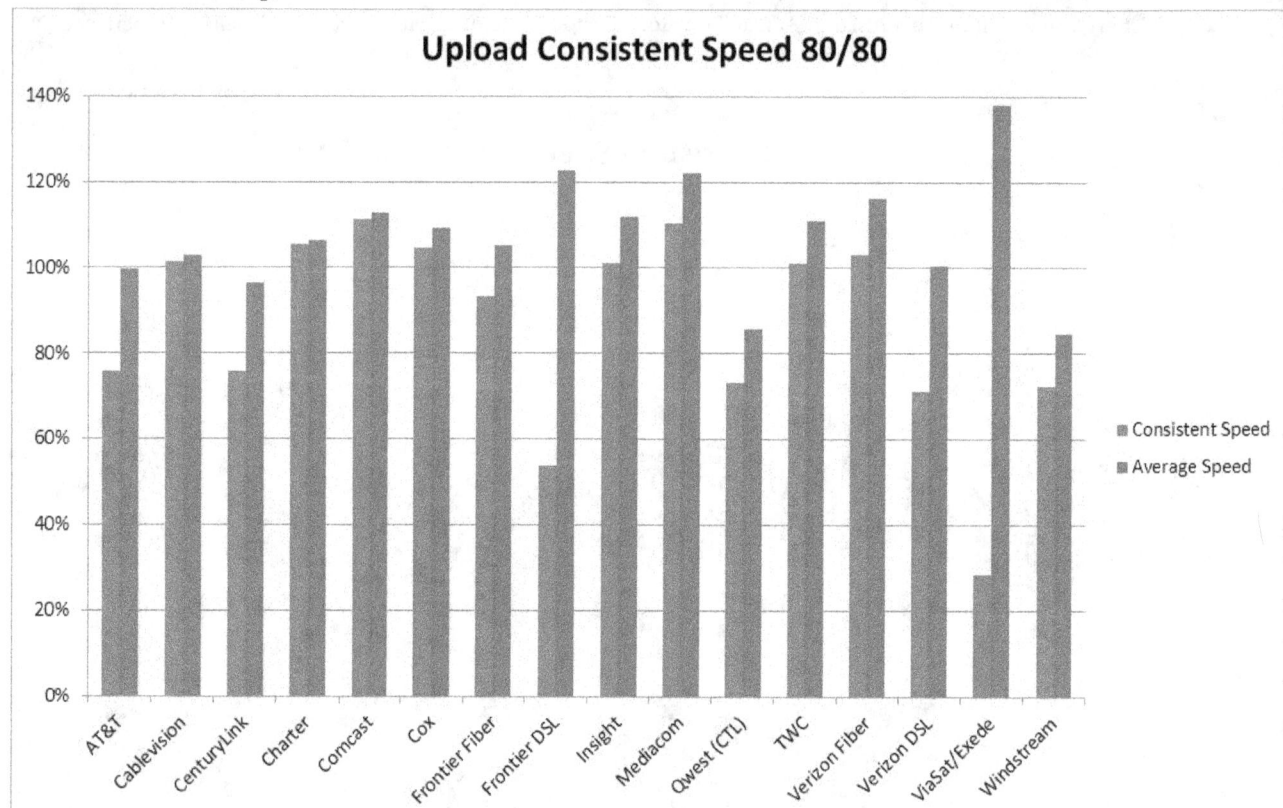

While only two ISPs achieved 100 percent or better of advertised download speeds at the 80%/80% level, 8 out of 15 ISPs achieved this for upload speeds. In our reporting we have consistently found that the ratio of actual to advertised speeds is consistently higher for upload than download speeds, possibly because the upload links see a lower utilization and congestion than download links.

VARIATIONS BY ACCESS TECHNOLOGY IN DELIVERY OF ADVERTISED SPEED

The delivery of advertised speeds also varied by technology. As shown in Chart 8, there is some variation by technology in actual versus advertised performance during peak periods. DSL on average meets 91 percent of advertised download speeds during peak periods; cable meets 102 percent; fiber-to-the-home meets 113 percent of advertised speeds; and satellite meets 139 percent of advertised download speed. During peak usage, ISPs are generally better at delivering advertised upload performance than download performance.[49]

Chart 8: Average Peak Period Sustained Download and Upload Speeds as a Percentage of Advertised, by Technology—September 2013 Test Data

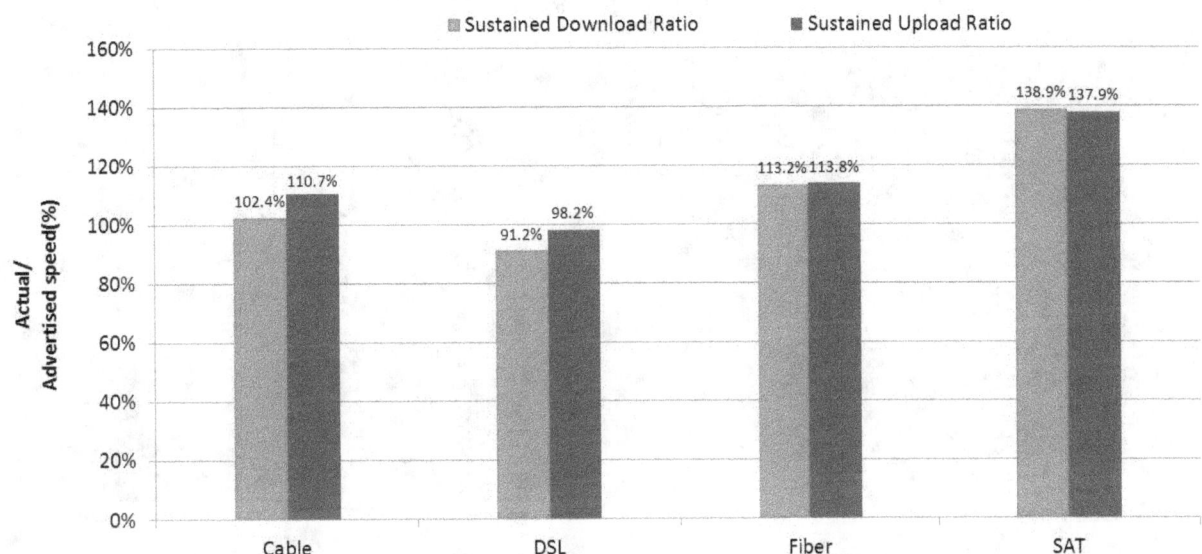

VARIATION BY SERVICE TIER IN DELIVERY OF ADVERTISED SPEED

Download Peak Period Throughput

As shown in Charts 9.1-9.5, peak usage period performance varies by service tier among ISPs included in this study during the September 2013 test period. On average, during peak periods, all ISPs deliver 80 percent or better with a majority of ISPs delivering performance 90 percent or better of advertised speeds. However, performance varies among service tiers. For example, Windstream's 1.5 Mbps tier delivers 78 percent of advertised speed, a low across all ISPs and speed tiers. In contrast, Windstream's best performing service tier of 6 Mbps tier delivers 90 percent of advertised speed. Other ISPs provide service that is either close to or exceeds advertised rates. In the 5-10 Mbps tier, all ISPs returned results that were significantly better than those from the previous year, with four providers showing similar improvements in the 12-15 Mbps speed tier.

Chart 9.1: Average Peak Period Sustained Download Speeds as a Percentage of Advertised, by Provider (1-5 Mbps Tier)—September 2013 Test Data

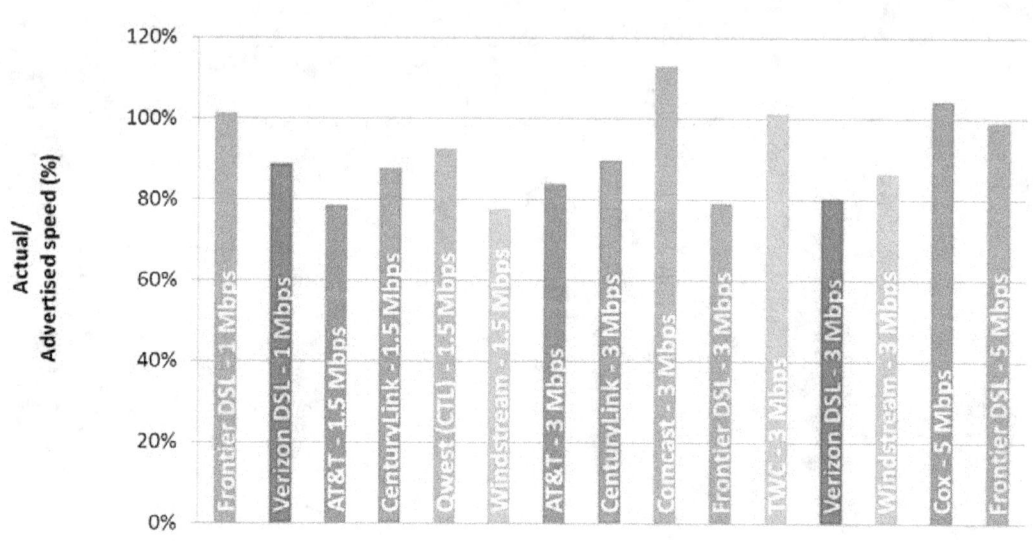

Chart 9.2: Average Peak Period Sustained Download Speeds as a Percentage of Advertised, by Provider (6-10 Mbps Tier)—September 2013 Test Data

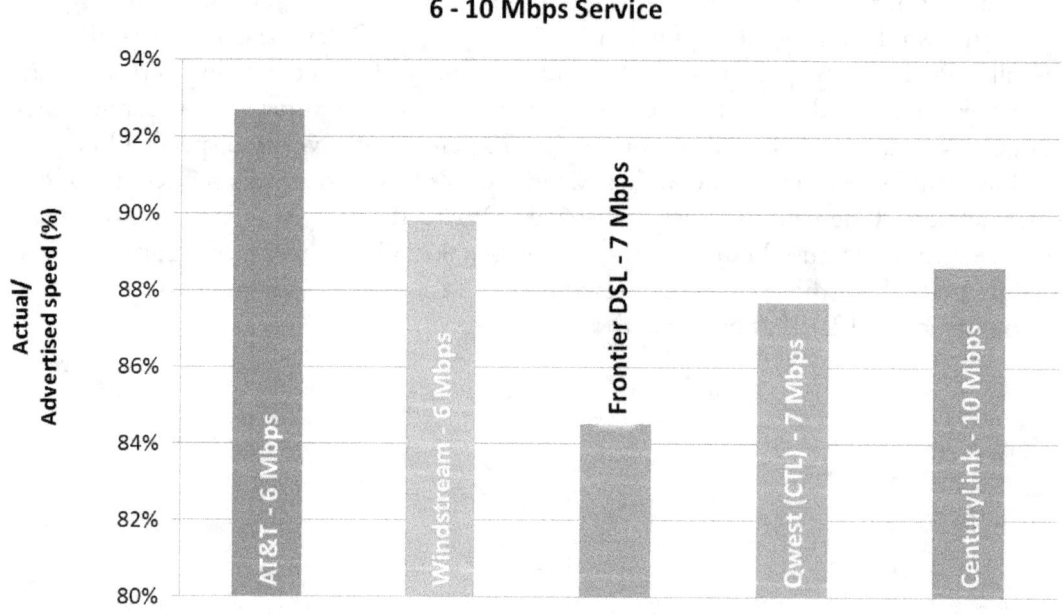

Chart 9.3: Average Peak Period Sustained Download Speeds as a Percentage of Advertised, by Provider (12-15 Mbps Tier)—September 2013 Test Data

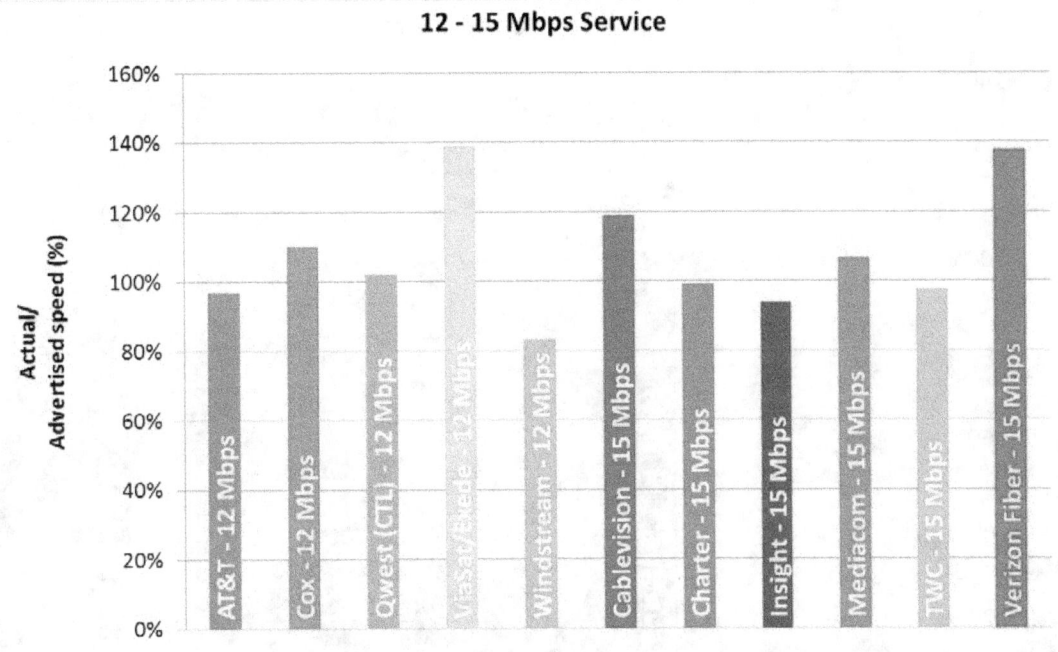

Chart 9.4: Average Peak Period Sustained Download Speeds as a Percentage of Advertised, by Provider (18-25 Mbps Tier)—September 2013 Test Data

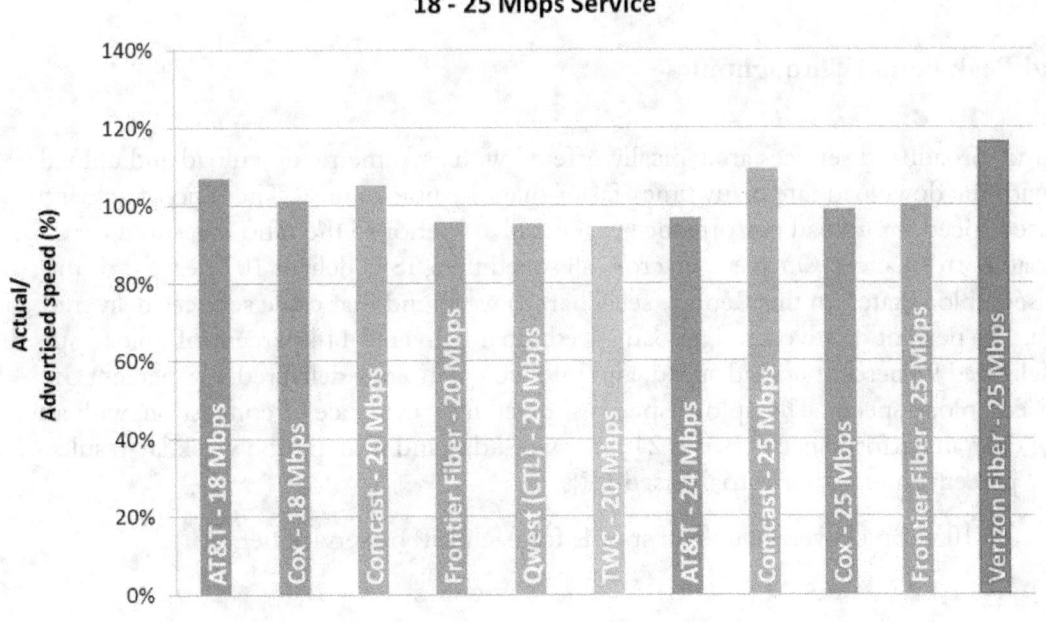

Chart 9.5: Average Peak Period Sustained Download Speeds as a Percentage of Advertised, by Provider (30-75 Mbps Tier)—September 2013 Test Data

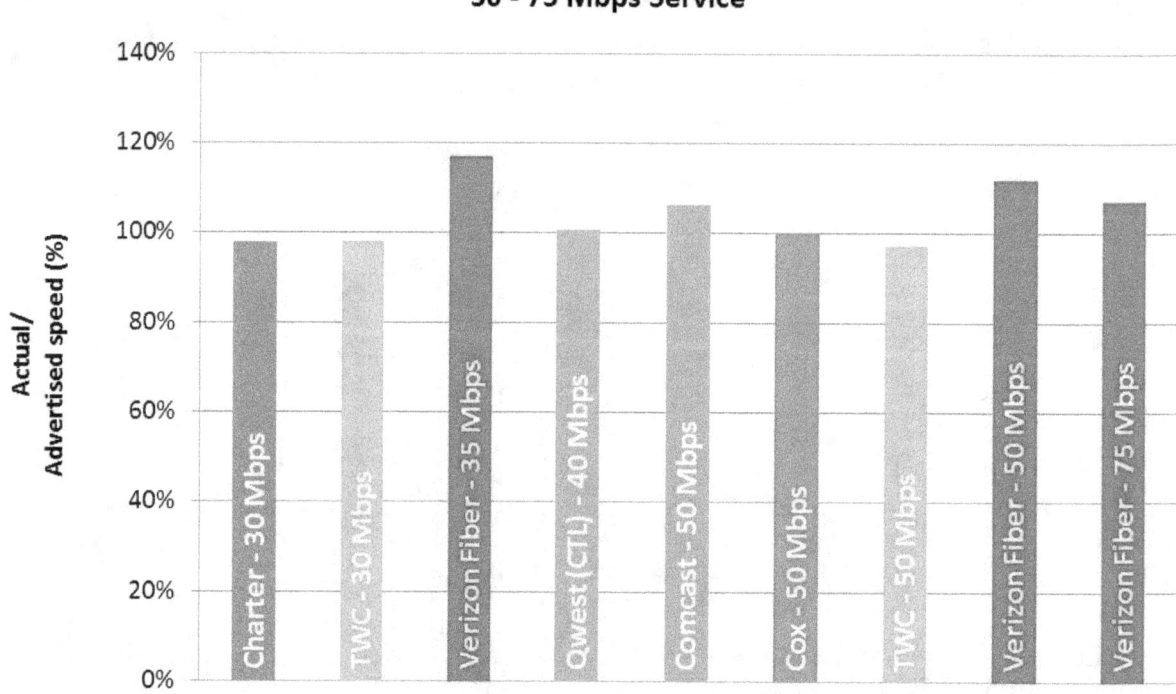

30 - 75 Mbps Service

Upload Peak Period Throughput

Consumer broadband services are typically offered with asymmetric download and upload rates, with the download rate many times faster than the upload rate. The ratio of actual to advertised speed for upload performance is generally superior to the ratio measured for download performance. On average across all speed tiers, ISPs deliver 107 percent of the advertised upload rate. In this Report (see Chart 8) we found that cable services delivered, on average, 111 percent of advertised upload speed; fiber delivered 114 percent of upload speed; DSL delivered 98 percent upload speed; and satellite technology delivered 138 percent of advertised upload speed. The upload speeds showed little evidence of congestion, with an average drop in performance between 24-hour week day and peak period weekday results of only 0.7 percent amongst terrestrial-based ISPs.

Charts 10.1-10.4 depict average upload speeds for each ISP by service tier.[50]

Chart 10.1: Average Peak Period Sustained Upload Speeds as a Percentage of Advertised, by Provider (0.256-0.64 Mbps Tier)—September 2013 Test Data

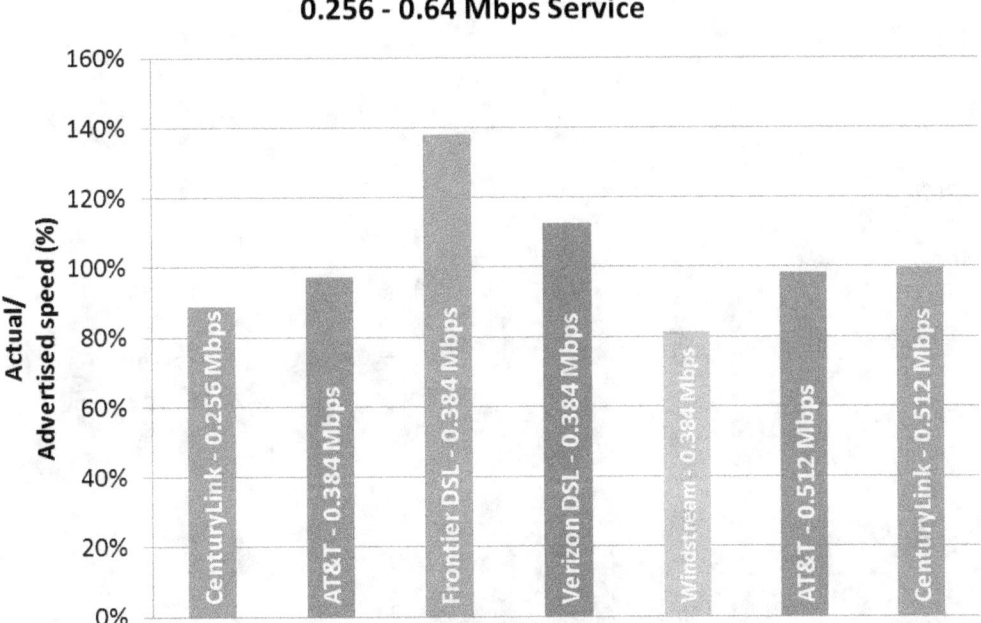

Chart 10.2: Average Peak Period Sustained Upload Speeds as a Percentage of Advertised, by Provider (0.768-1.5 Mbps Tier)—September 2013 Test Data

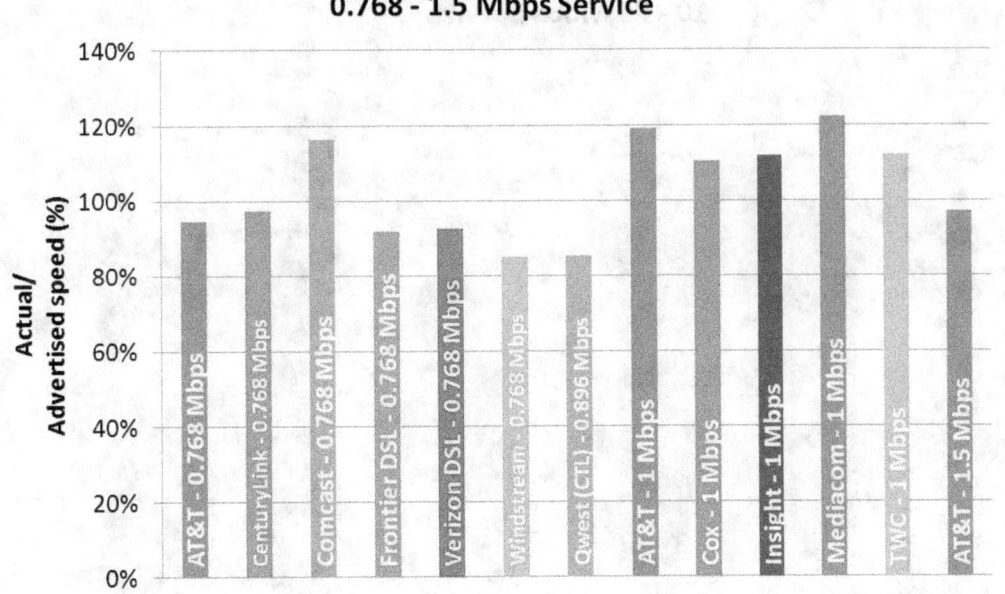

Chart 10.3: Average Peak Period Sustained Upload Speeds as a Percentage of Advertised, by Provider (2-5 Mbps Tier)—September 2013 Test Data

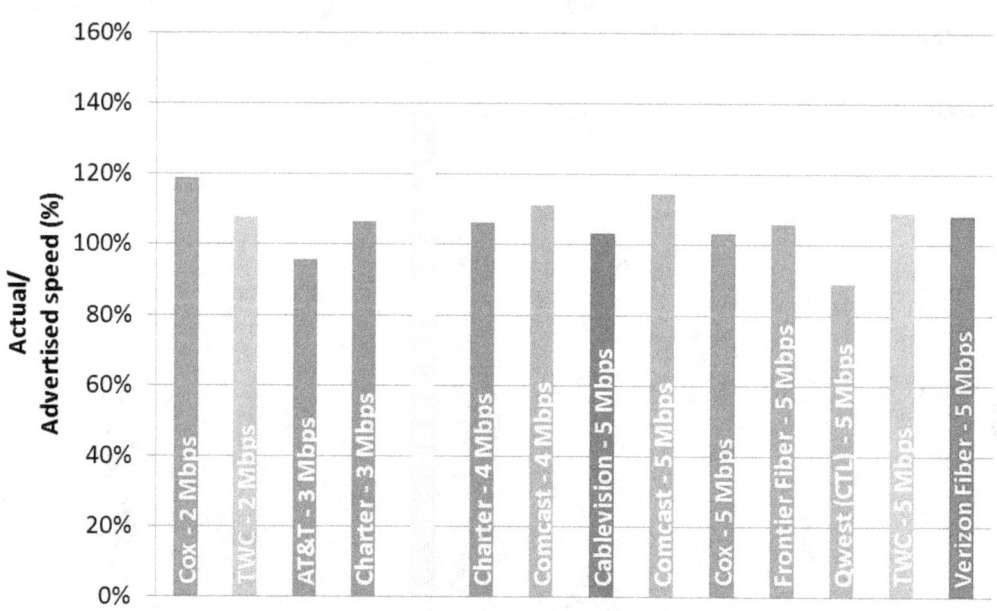

Chart 10.4: Average Peak Period Sustained Upload Speeds as a Percentage of Advertised, by Provider (10-35 Mbps Tier)—September 2013 Test Data

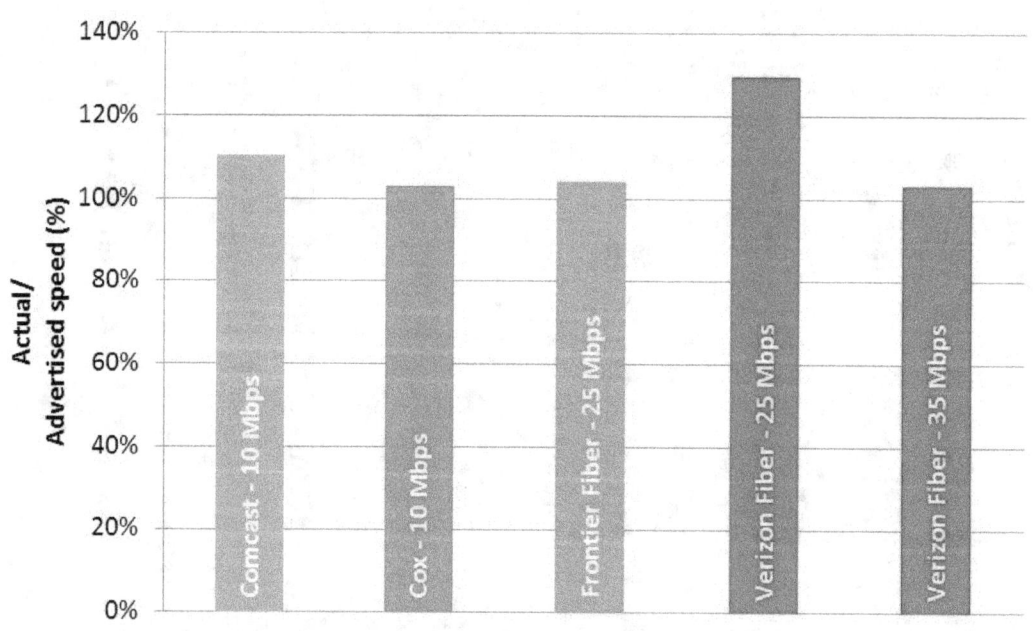

Burst Versus Sustained Download Throughput

Comparing burst download speeds versus advertised speeds demonstrates the effect that burst services can have on data throughput. To test for the possible effect of burst technology, we compare the average speed performance in the first five seconds of a speed test to the average speed performance in the last five seconds of a total 30 second test. Large differences may indicate the use of burst technology, while smaller differences are likely the effect of variable packet performance. Not all ISPs use burst technology and inclusion of an ISP in Chart 11 does not necessarily indicate that burst technology is employed, merely that that variability in performance from the beginning to the end of a speed test exceeded a filter threshold of ten percent.[51] We note that in comparison with last year's report, the overall impact of burst technology has markedly declined.

Chart 11 below shows the results of our burst test.[52] Results that showed a less than 10 percent improvement were discarded to make the chart easier to read. Unlike previous years where burst technology was seen to temporarily increase performance by as much as 79 percent, this year fewer providers employed burst technology and those carriers who did employ it saw gains that were relatively smaller than in previous years, particularly at the higher speed tiers. This may be a consequence of the migration of consumers to higher speeds where burst technology seems to have less effect.

Chart 11: Average Peak Period Burst Download Speeds as a Percentage Increase over Sustained Download Speeds, by Provider Where Tiers Showed a Greater than 10 Percent Increase—September 2013 Test Data

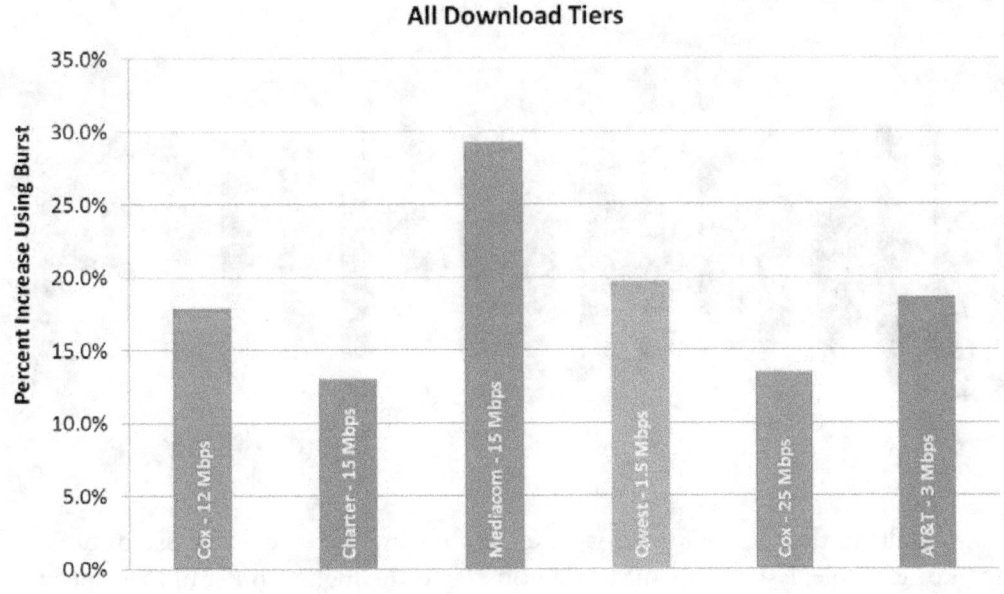

The use of transient performance boosting features is even less prevalent for upstream connections, with only three carriers using it at extremely low speeds (0.25 Mbps to 2 Mbps).

Chart 12: Average Peak Period Burst Upload Speeds as a Percentage Increase over Sustained Download Speeds, by Provider (All Tiers)—September 2013 Test Data

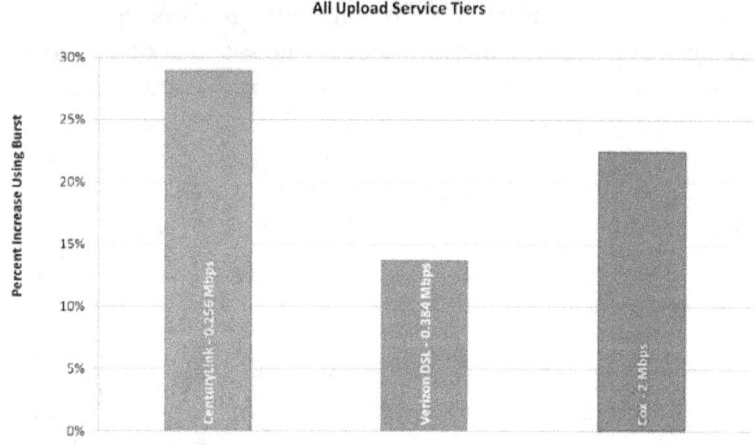

Chart 13 provides an overview of the average burst download and upload speed per ISP as a percent of advertised performance. Most ISPs do not employ a burst feature, so the results for many ISPs will not differ markedly from their sustained speed performance.

Chart 13: Average Peak Period Burst Download and Upload Speeds as a Percentage of Sustained Speed, by Provider—September 2013 Test Data

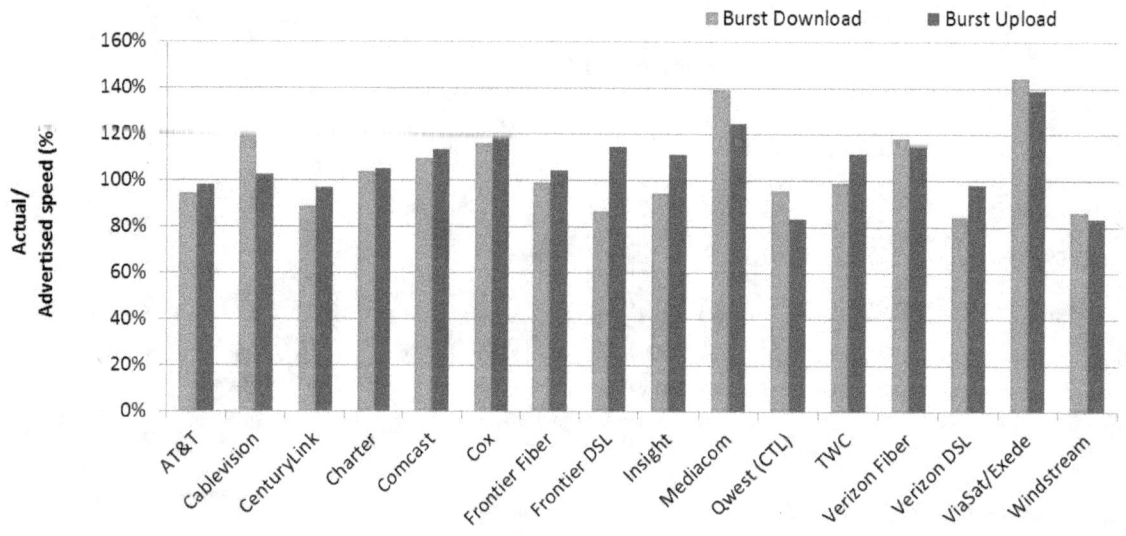

In comparing results to the previous years we see a significant decrease in the use of burst technology. For example, last year Comcast demonstrated the highest burst upload speed, reaching on average across all speed tiers 168 percent of advertised upload speed, while for download speed Comcast, Mediacom and TWC showed increases of over 140 percent of advertised speed. This year Comcast showed only 113 percent of advertised download speed based on the burst speed measurement methodology.) Only Mediacom retained its burst speed increase of 140 percent this year.

Latency

Latency test results in the September 2013 testing period showed an increase from the February 2013 Report. This is likely due, in part, to the changes to our measurement architecture discussed earlier. As can be seen from Chart 14, latency varies by technology and by service tier.[53] However, this relationship is complex. For example, average latency within a technology class is largely invariant within a range of speed tiers, although in general higher speed tiers have lower latency than lower tiers. The largest influences affecting latency are technology driven. We continue to believe that for properly engineered networks the primary causes of latency are intrinsic to the service architecture and are primarily determined by load independent effects.

Fiber-to-the-home, on average, had the best performance in terms of latency, with 24 ms average during the peak period. Cable had 30 ms latency, and DSL had 48 ms latency. The highest average latency in a speed tier for a terrestrial technology was for DSL with 54 ms measured latency. The highest latency recorded for a single ISP using terrestrial technology was 63 ms. Satellite technology, due to the distances between the satellite and terrestrial points, recorded the highest overall latency of 671 ms.[54] While the test results found variance in latencies among technologies, the latencies measured here for all of the terrestrial-based technologies should be adequate for common latency-sensitive Internet applications, such as VoIP.[55] As noted, the situation is more complex for satellite, and dependent on a number of factors, including application sensitivity to latency and user perception of latency's effects.

Chart 14: Average Peak Period Latency in Milliseconds, by Technology—September 2013 Test Data

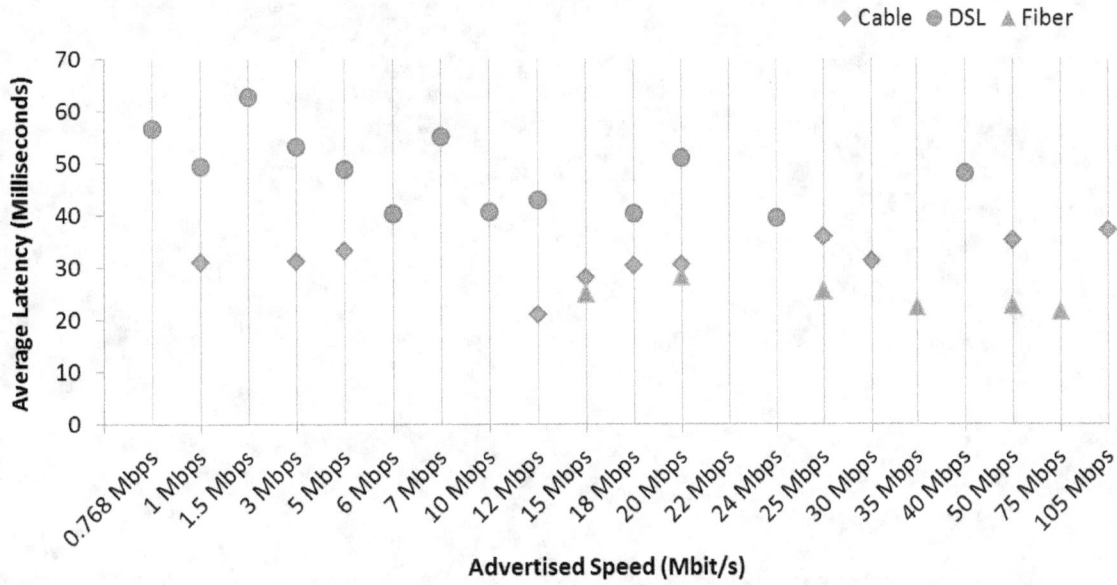

Charts 15.1-15.5 display average web page loading[56] time by speed tier. Web pages load much

faster as broadband speed increases, but beyond 15 Mbps, performance increases for basic web browsing diminish dramatically. The data indicate that a consumer subscribing to a 10 Mbps speed tier is unlikely to experience a significant performance increase in basic web browsing—*e.g.*, accessing web pages, but not streaming video or using other high-bandwidth applications such as video chat—by moving to a higher speed tier. These results are largely consistent with, and show no significant improvement over, previous results.

Chart 15.1: Web Loading Time by Advertised Speed, by Technology (1-3 Mbps Tier)—September 2013 Test Data

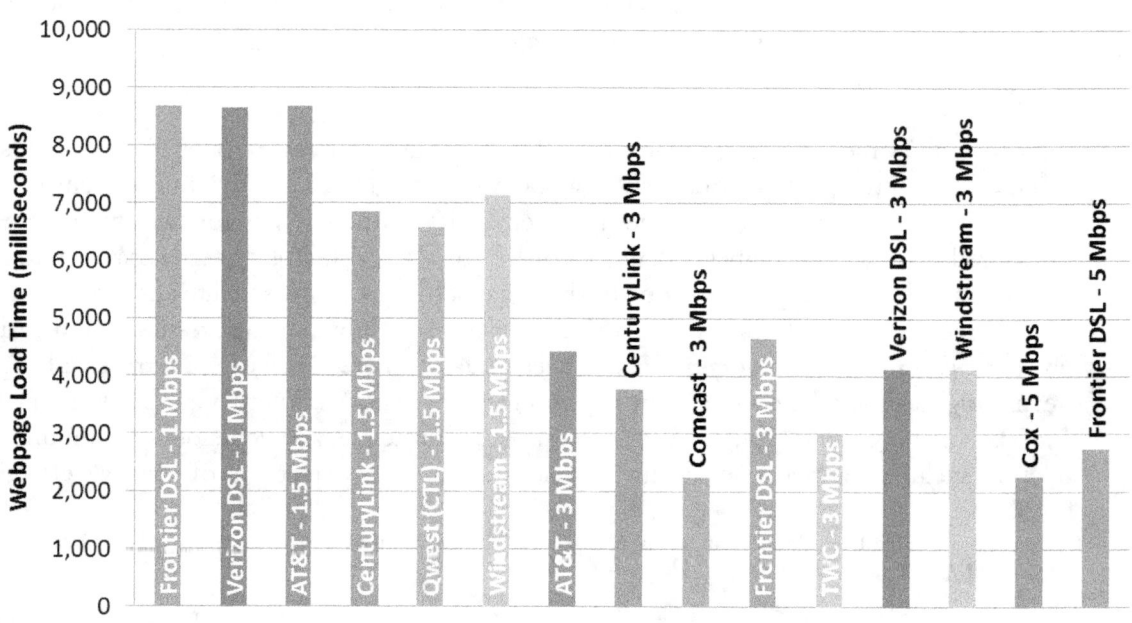

Chart 15.2: Web Loading Time by Advertised Speed, by Technology (6-10 Mbps Tier)—September 2013 Test Data

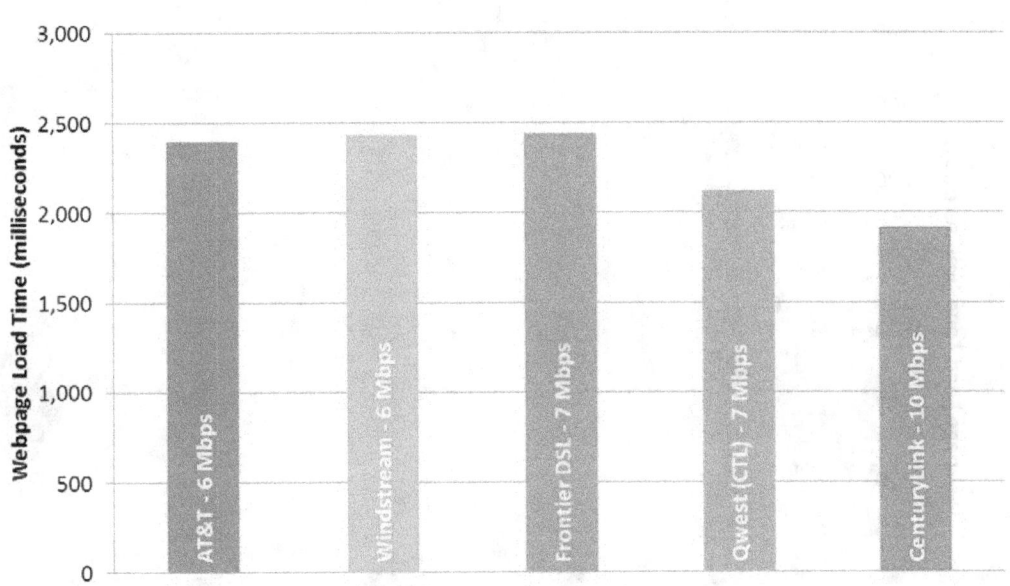

6 - 10 Mbps Service

Chart 15.3: Web Loading Time by Advertised Speed, by Technology (12-15 Mbps Tier)—September 2013 Test Data

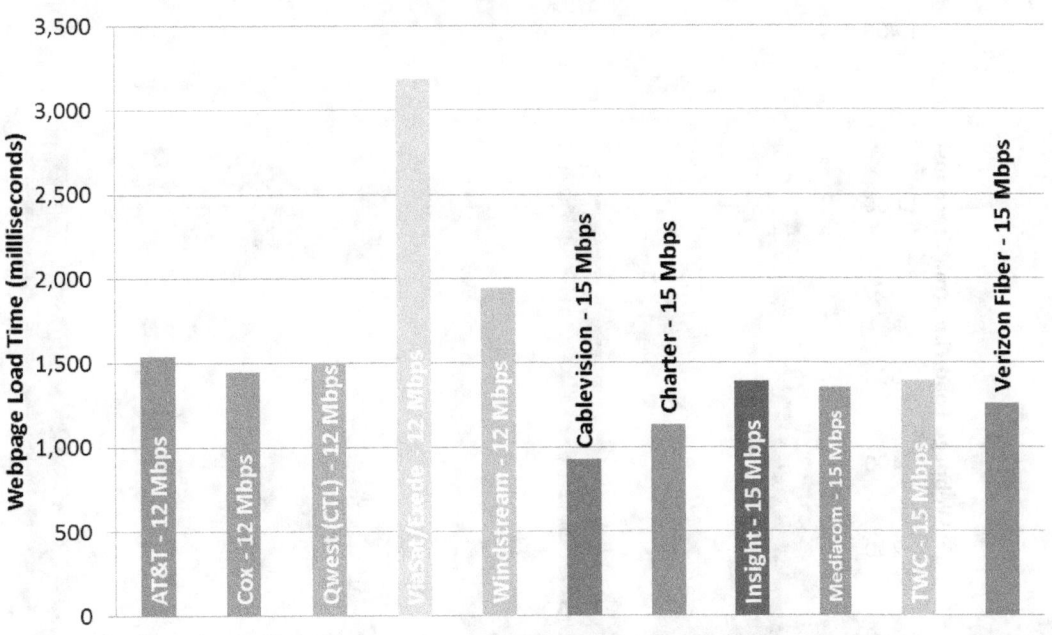

12 - 15 Mbps Service

Chart 15.4: Web Loading Time by Advertised Speed, by Technology (18-25 Mbps Tier)—September 2013 Test Data

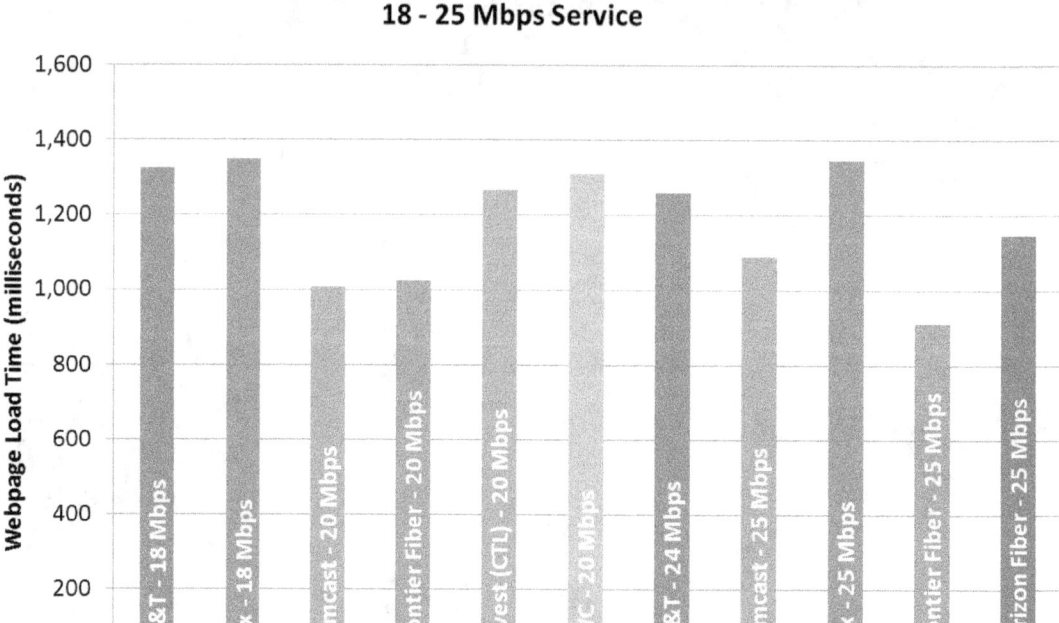

18 - 25 Mbps Service

Chart 15.5: Web Loading Time by Advertised Speed, by Technology (30-75 Mbps Tier)—September 2013 Test Data

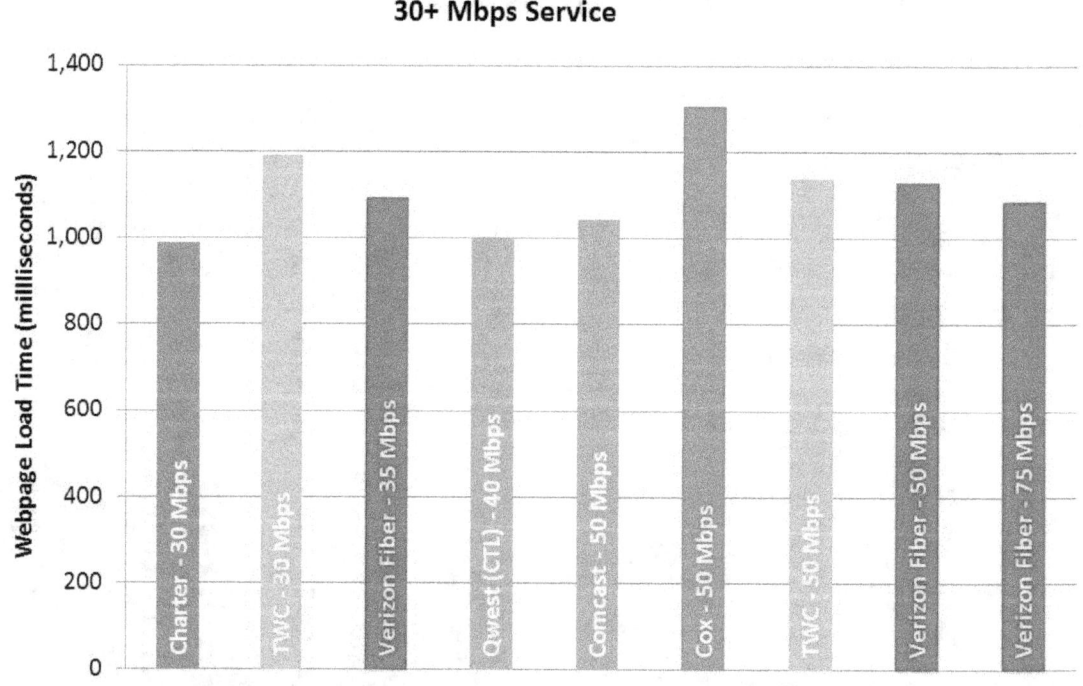

30+ Mbps Service

Chart 16 shows in a consistent scale across all speed tiers the effect of increasing speed on web loading time. As can be seen in this chart, as speed first increases, there is a steep drop in web loading times, which levels off at about 15 Mbps. Beyond that speed, web page loading time decreases only slightly.

Chart 16: Web Loading Time by Advertised Speed (1-75 Mbps Tier)—September 2013 Test Data

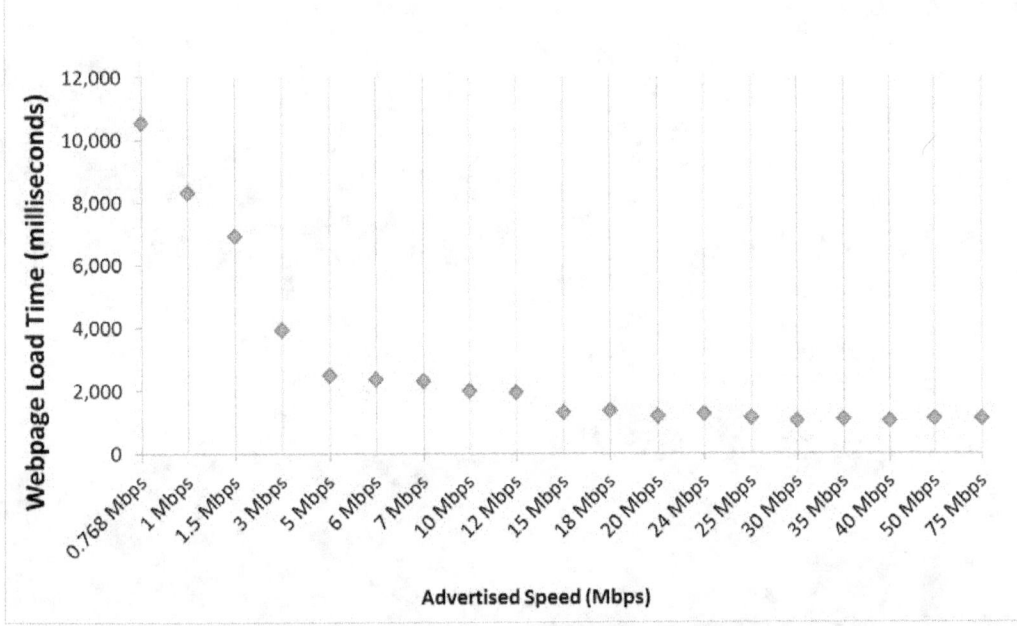

VARIATION BY TIME OF DAY

Chart 17 shows that day-time performance varied for most technologies. During idle periods there was more capacity available for the consumer, while at peak usage periods available capacity per consumer diminished. As noted above, since the initiation of this program the participating ISPs, on average, have both improved performance and have provided more reliable estimates of actual speeds to consumers. As a result, overall ISP performance has become increasingly consistent.

Chart 17: Hourly Sustained Download Speeds as a Percentage of Advertised, by Provider—September 2013 Test Data

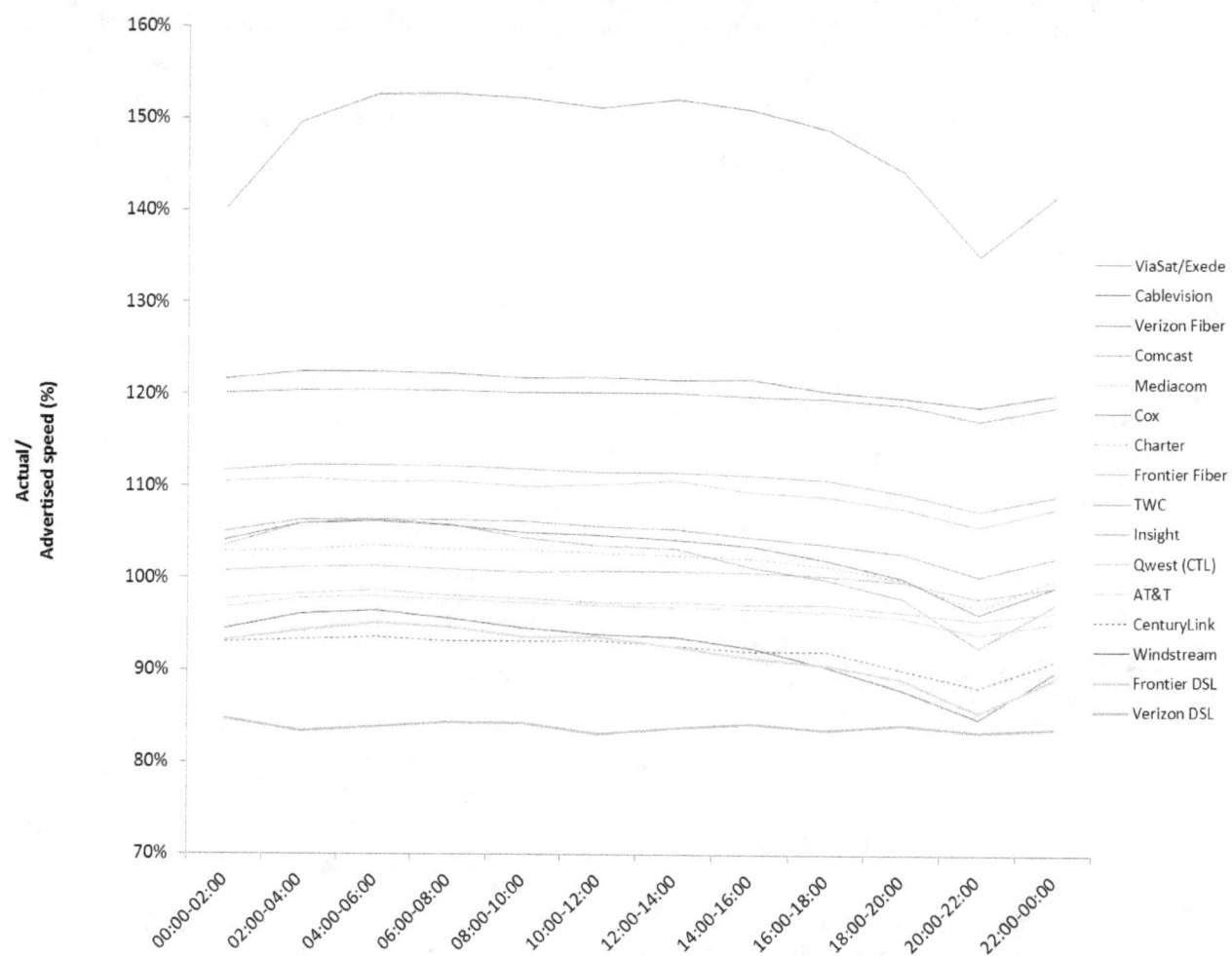

24 HOUR VERSUS PEAK PERFORMANCE VARIATION BY TECHNOLOGY

Chart 18 compares the average hour-by-hour download speed performance for fiber, cable, DSL, and satellite technologies to the 24-hour average speed for each technology. Performance of all technologies fluctuates slightly during the day. For example, while cable technology has a daily 24-hour average speed of slightly over 100 percent of advertised rates, it achieves this by delivering slightly higher than average performance during non-peak hours and slightly lower performance during peak periods.

Chart 18: Average Sustained Download Speeds as a Percentage of Advertised Over a 24-Hour Period, by Technology—September 2013 Test Data

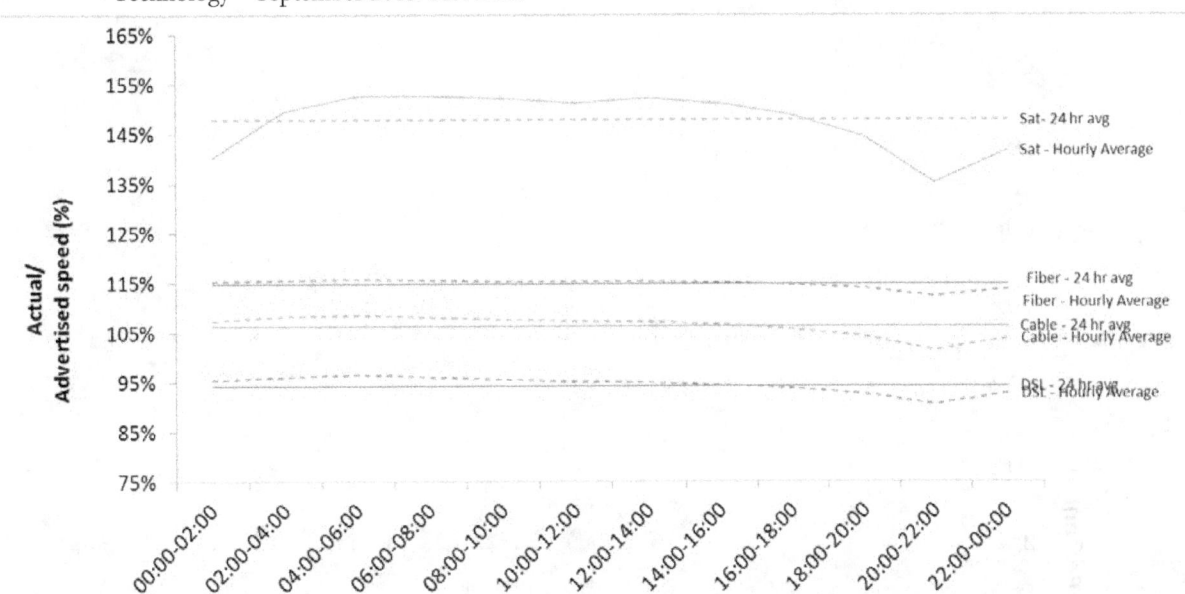

CUMULATIVE DISTRIBUTION FOR DOWNLOAD SPEEDS

The cumulative distribution charts provide some illustration of how broadband performance varies within the sample population. In theory, test results for a particular ISP could return an average performance level that was achieved while performance varied greatly across subscribers. For example, an ISP that delivered well over 100 percent of advertised speed to some subscribers might deliver well under 100 percent of advertised speed to other subscribers and still deliver, on average, 100 percent of advertised speed. The cumulative distribution accounts for this by showing the percent of subscribers to a particular speed tier whose average speed is equal to or greater than the indicated value for that percentage. For example, if the 90th percentile of the chart intersected with 80 percent of advertised speed, it would indicate that 90 percent of the population is receiving, on average, performance of 80 percent or better of advertised speed and that the remaining 10 percent of the population is receiving an average speed less than 80 percent of advertised speed. (This differs from our consistent speed measure, which shows the minimum speed a percentage of all consumers receive for an indicated fraction of time.) We believe that the cumulative distribution charts below provide some reassurance that large variations across subscribers are not resulting in misleading averages. Chart 19 shows that, at the 80th percentile, fiber consumers are receiving 102 percent or better of advertised rates, cable consumers are receiving 102 percent or better, satellite consumers 147 percent of advertised rates, and DSL consumers are receiving 84 percent or better of advertised rates. At the 90th percentile, fiber consumers are receiving 99 percent or better of advertised rates, cable consumers are receiving 98 percent, satellite 141 percent, and DSL consumers 72 percent of advertised rates.

Chart 19: Cumulative Distribution of Sustained Download Speeds as a Percentage of Advertised Speed, by Technology—September 2013 Test Data

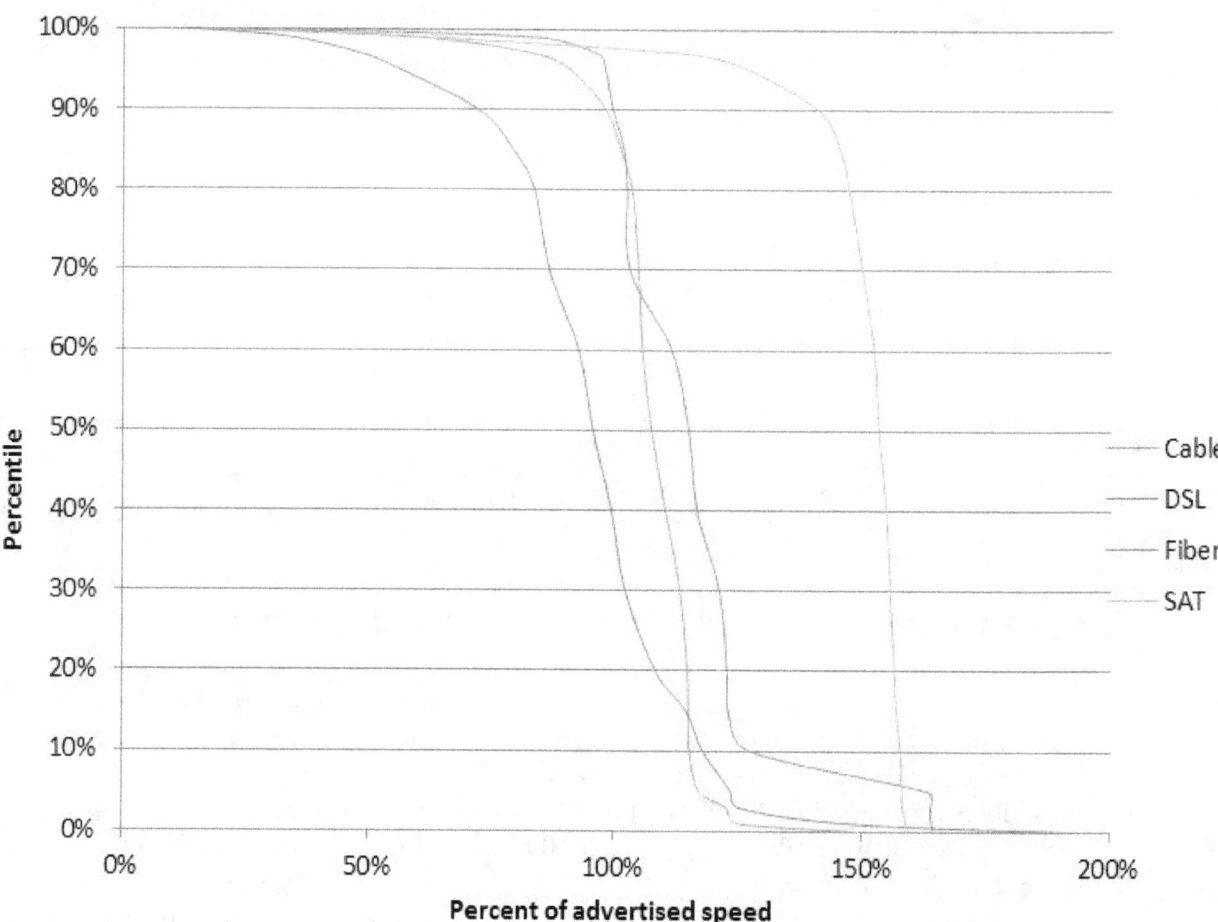

Charts 20.1-20.2 show the cumulative distribution of sustained download speeds by provider. To clarify the data, we have divided the performance of the sixteen ISPs technology categories into two charts, with the providers divided by alphabet.

Chart 20.1: Cumulative Distribution of Sustained Download Speeds as a Percentage of Advertised Speed, by Provider (9 Providers)—September 2013 Test Data

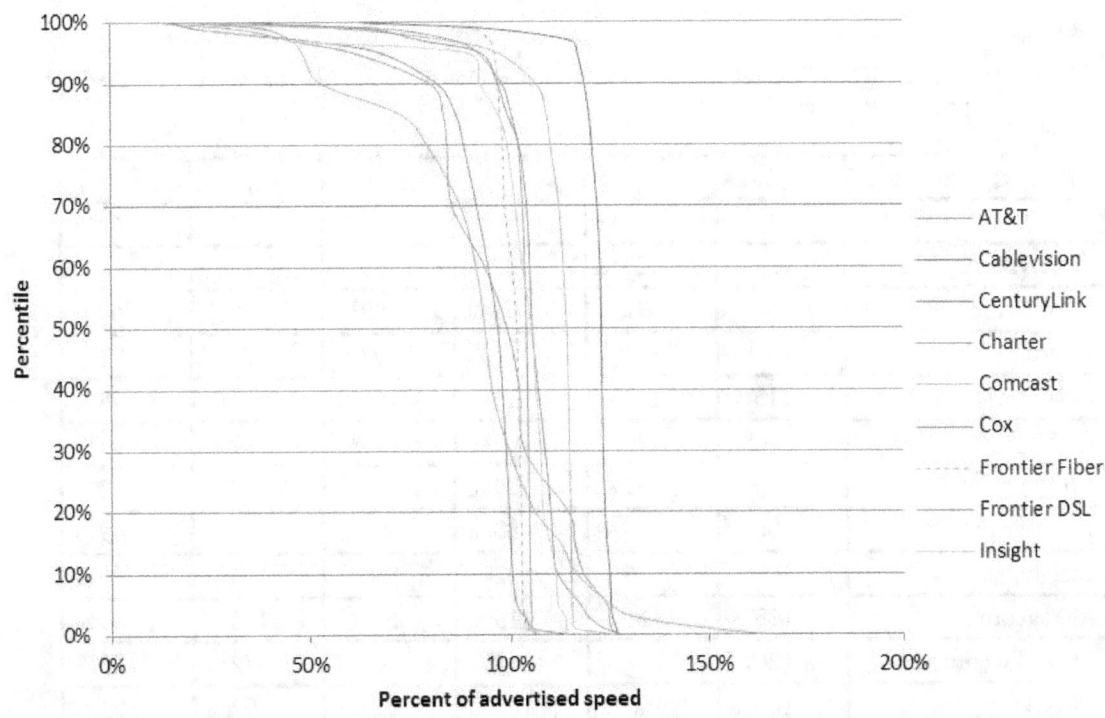

Chart 20.2: Cumulative Distribution of Sustained Download Speeds as a Percentage of Advertised Speed, by Provider (7 providers)—September 2013 Test Data

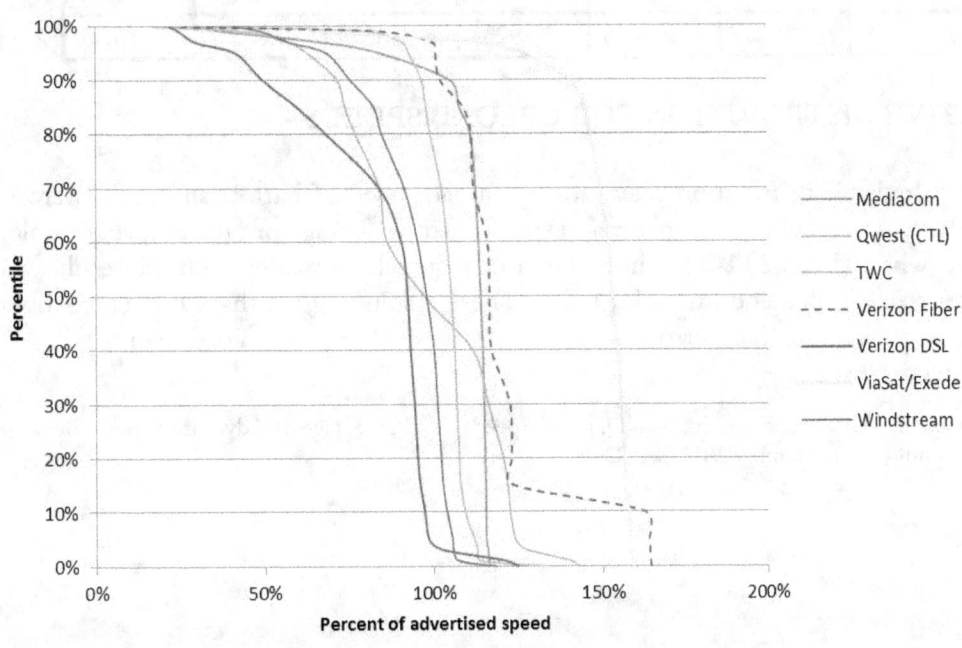

For easier readability, we have also included the CDF data illustrated in Charts 20.1-20.2 as Figure 1.

Figure 1: Cumulative Distribution Percentiles for Sustained Download Speeds as a Percentage of Advertised Speed, by Provider

	20%	50%	70%	80%	90%	95%
AT&T	115%	99%	86%	85%	81%	62%
Cablevision	124%	123%	122%	121%	119%	117%
CenturyLink	100%	97%	92%	89%	82%	68%
Charter	105%	104%	103%	102%	98%	93%
Comcast	115%	114%	113%	111%	107%	98%
Cox	110%	106%	105%	103%	97%	93%
Frontier Fiber	103%	102%	99%	99%	97%	97%
Frontier DSL	106%	94%	88%	80%	53%	49%
Insight	108%	106%	102%	100%	93%	90%
Mediacom	115%	114%	113%	111%	105%	84%
Qwest/Centurylink	120%	97%	84%	77%	72%	63%
TWC	108%	106%	103%	99%	97%	93%
Verizon Fiber	123%	117%	112%	111%	102%	101%
Verizon DSL	95%	92%	84%	69%	50%	42%
ViaSat/Exede	157%	153%	150%	147%	141%	126%
Windstream	102%	98%	92%	85%	76%	69%

CUMULATIVE DISTRIBUTION FOR UPLOAD SPEEDS

As with the cumulative distribution charts for download speeds, Chart 21 shows the percent of subscribers to a particular speed tier who experienced an average or greater level of upload performance, while Charts 22.1-22.2 show the same results by provider, with the results again split into two charts alphabetically for legibility. These results suggest that DSL, cable, fiber, and satellite return even higher performance, with fewer outliers, for upload than for download speeds.

Chart 21: Cumulative Distribution of Sustained Upload Speeds as a Percentage of Advertised Speed, by Technology—September 2013 Test Data

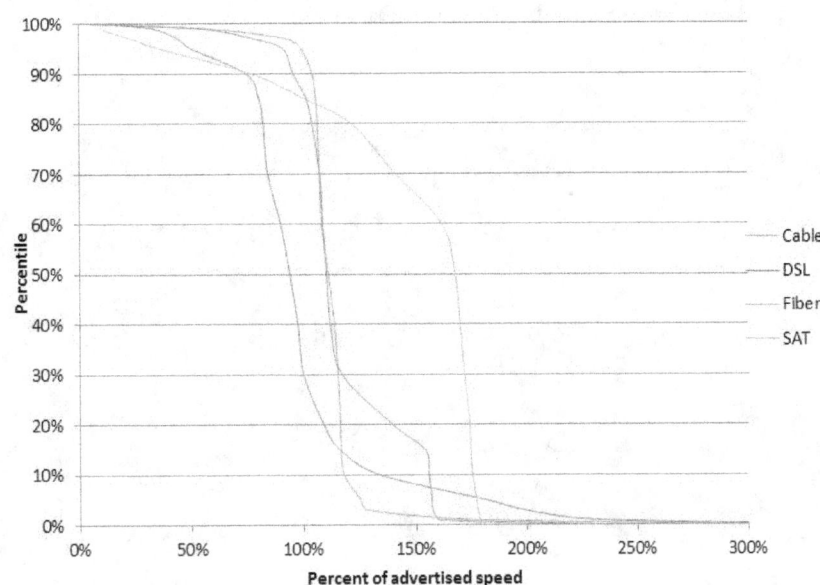

Chart 22.1: Cumulative Distribution of Sustained Upload Speeds as a Percentage of Advertised Speed, by Provider (9 Providers)—September 2013 Test Data

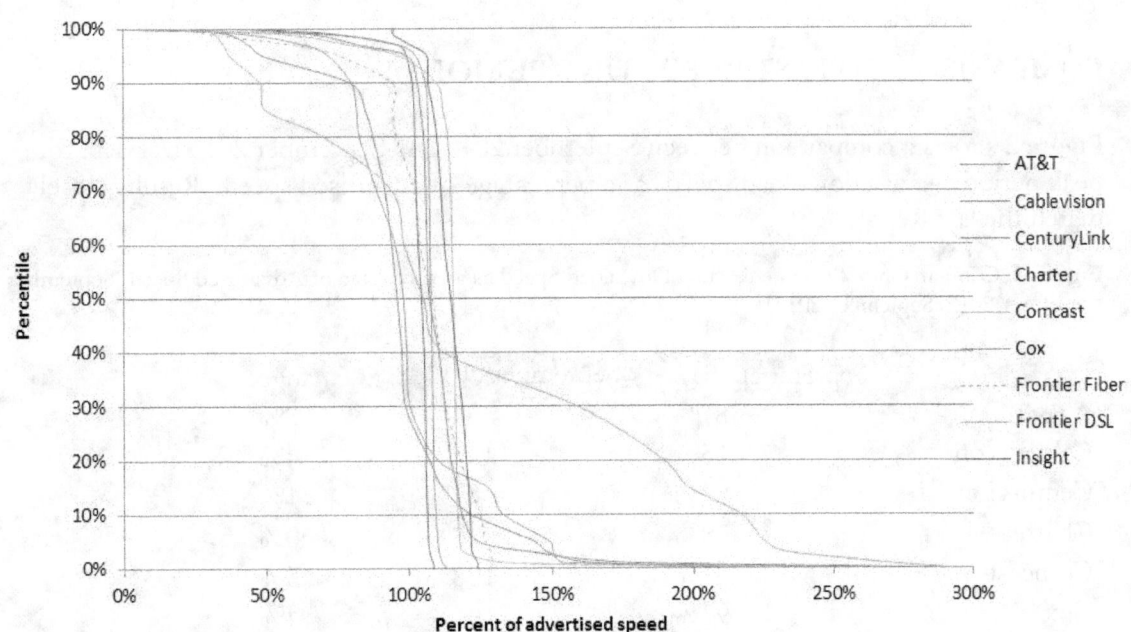

Chart 22.2: Cumulative Distribution of Sustained Upload Speeds as a Percentage of Advertised Speed, by Provider (7 Providers)—September 2013 Test Data

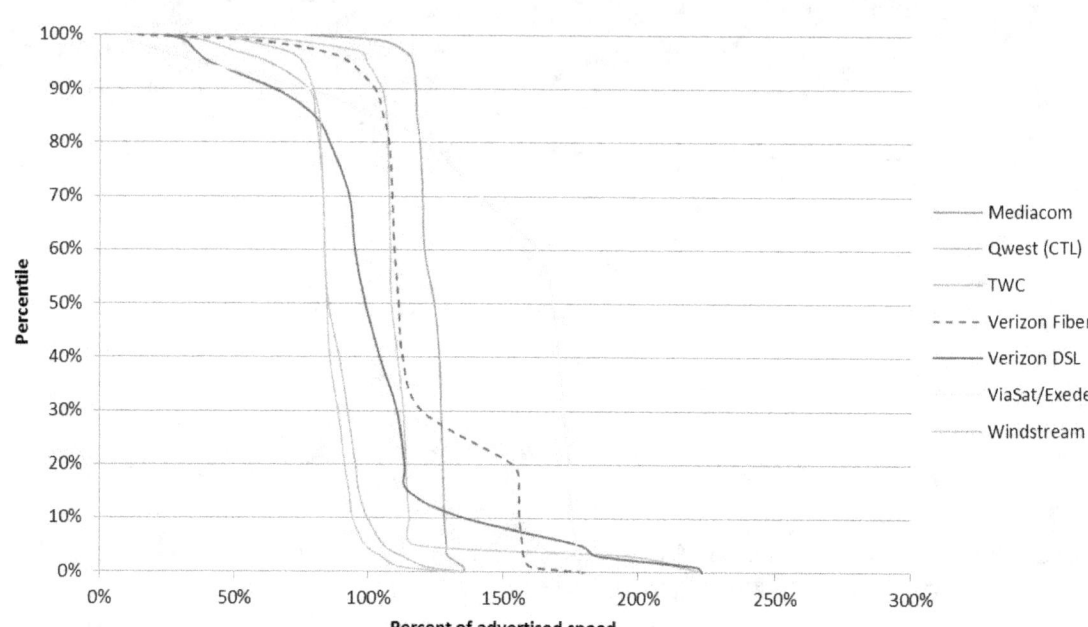

COMPARISON TO LAST REPORTING PERIOD

Figure 2 shows a comparison between September 2012 and September 2013 test data for peak period average download speeds as a percentage of advertised speed. Results closely match the last Report.

Figure 2: Comparison of Sustained Actual Download Speed as a Percentage of Advertised Speed (September 2012/September 2013)

ISP	September 2012	September 2013	% Change
AT&T	87%	94%	8%
Cablevision	115%	119%	4%
CenturyLink	87%	89%	1%
Charter	98%	98%	0%
Comcast	103%	108%	5%
Cox	97%	101%	4%
Frontier Fiber*	Not available	99%	-
Frontier DSL*	87%	86%	-1%
Insight	85%	94%	11%
Mediacom	99%	107%	8%
Qwest (CTL)	82%	95%	16%

TWC	94%	97%	4%
Verizon (Fiber)	118%	117%	-1%
Verizon (DSL)	88%	83%	-5%
ViaSat/Exede	137%	139%	1%
Windstream	81%	86%	5%

*Last year's Report did not split Frontier subscribers into Frontier Fiber and Frontier DSL groups. The 87 percent value was an average that accounted for both fiber and DSL technologies; most subscribers used DSL.

ACTUAL VERSUS ADVERTISED SPEEDS

Figure 3 below lists the advertised speed tiers included in this study, and compares this with the actual average peak performance results from September 2013. As before, we note that the actual sustained download speeds here were based on national averages, and should not be taken to represent the performance experienced by any one consumer in any specific market for these ISPs.

Figure 3: Peak Period Sustained Download Performance, by Provider—September 2013 Test Data

Actual Sustained Download Speed (Mbps)	Advertised Download Speed Tier	Provider	Actual Sustained Speed / Advertised Speed Tier
1.01	1 Mbps	Frontier (DSL)	101%
0.89	1 Mbps	Verizon (DSL)	89%
1.18	1.5 Mbps	AT&T	79%
1.32	1.5 Mbps	CenturyLink	88%
1.39	1.5 Mbps	Qwest (CTL)	93%
1.16	1.5 Mbps	Windstream	78%
2.52	3 Mbps	AT&T	84%
2.69	3 Mbps	CenturyLink	90%
3.39	3 Mbps	Comcast	113%
2.37	3 Mbps	Frontier (DSL)	79%
3.03	3 Mbps	TWC	101%
2.41	3 Mbps	Verizon (DSL)	80%

Actual Sustained Download Speed (Mbps)	Advertised Download Speed Tier	Provider	Actual Sustained Speed / Advertised Speed Tier
2.59	3 Mbps	Windstream	86%
5.21	5 Mbps	Cox	104%
4.96	5 Mbps	Frontier (DSL)	99%
5.56	6 Mbps	AT&T	93%
5.39	6 Mbps	Windstream	90%
5.92	7 Mbps	Frontier (DSL)	85%
6.14	7 Mbps	Qwest (CTL)	88%
8.86	10 Mbps	CenturyLink	89%
11.63	12 Mbps	AT&T	97%
13.21	12 Mbps	Cox	110%
12.27	12 Mbps	Qwest (CTL)	102%
16.66	12 Mbps	ViaSat/Exede	139%
9.97	12 Mbps	Windstream	83%
17.81	15 Mbps	Cablevision	119%
14.87	15 Mbps	Charter	99%
14.07	15 Mbps	Insight	94%
16.03	15 Mbps	Mediacom	107%
14.63	15 Mbps	TWC	98%
20.67	15 Mbps	Verizon (fiber)	138%
19.25	18 Mbps	AT&T	107%
18.22	18 Mbps	Cox	101%
21.07	20 Mbps	Comcast	105%
19.16	20 Mbps	Frontier (fiber)	96%

Actual Sustained Download Speed (Mbps)	Advertised Download Speed Tier	Provider	Actual Sustained Speed / Advertised Speed Tier
19.05	20 Mbps	Qwest (CTL)	95%
18.88	20 Mbps	TWC	94%
23.20	24 Mbps	AT&T	97%
27.33	25 Mbps	Comcast	109%
24.75	25 Mbps	Cox	99%
25.01	25 Mbps	Frontier (Fiber)	100%
29.09	25 Mbps	Verizon (Fiber)	116%
29.37	30 Mbps	Charter	98%
29.41	30 Mbps	TWC	98%
40.96	35 Mbps	Verizon (Fiber)	117%
40.27	40 Mbps	Qwest (CTL)	101%
53.21	50 Mbps	Comcast	106%
50.11	50 Mbps	Cox	100%
48.69	50 Mbps	TWC	97%
55.93	50 Mbps	Verizon (Fiber)	112%
80.28	75 Mbps	Verizon (Fiber)	107%

DATA CONSUMPTION

Test traffic data use is tracked and subtracted from each consumer panelist's personal data usage, which allows us to include a chart demonstrating consumer data consumption. The data was taken from a subset of 5760 measurement devices that were active during the measurement period,[57] which reported a total of 301 terabytes[58] of data consumed, which represents the amount of data uploaded and downloaded through all measurement devices across the panel, minus traffic associated with the program. Chart 23 shows the average amount of data traffic consumed by users in each speed tier, normalized as a percentage of total traffic generated by all consumers.[59] This normalized view of user traffic shows a correlation between data consumption and speed tiers. In general, we found a correlation between higher speed tiers and greater data consumption by the average user. This could mean that, as higher speeds are made available to consumers, consumers increase the amount of data they consume through some combination of greater use of the Internet and adoption of more data-intensive applications and services, or that consumers who use more data-intensive applications on the Internet tend to subscribe to faster speed tiers.

Chart 23: Normalized Average User Traffic—September 2013 Test Data

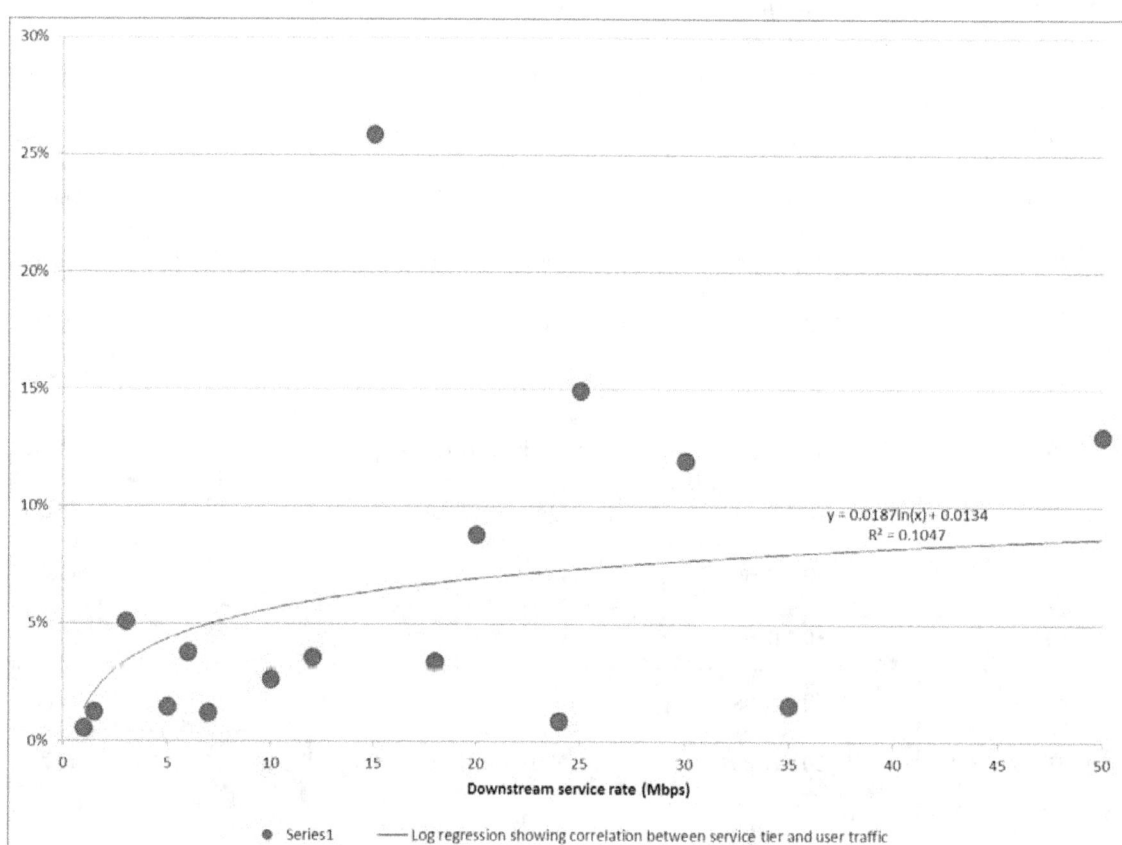

Chart 24 shows the cumulative distribution of traffic by technology. One important note about the data consumption information presented in this Report: the panel methodology specifically attempted to exclude both users with high consumption profiles and very fast tiers that had relatively low subscription rates. For these and other reasons, while the data do show a correlation between speed tier and data consumption, no conclusions can be drawn about total data consumption by broadband subscribers. In other words, while Chart 24 does not show data consumption above roughly 160 GB, that does not mean that typical broadband subscribers do not consume more than that amount each month, just that such subscribers would be excluded by the methodology of the Report. In addition, data consumption within the sample population has increased from the previous study[60].

Chart 24: Cumulative Distribution of User Traffic, by Technology—September 2013 Test Data

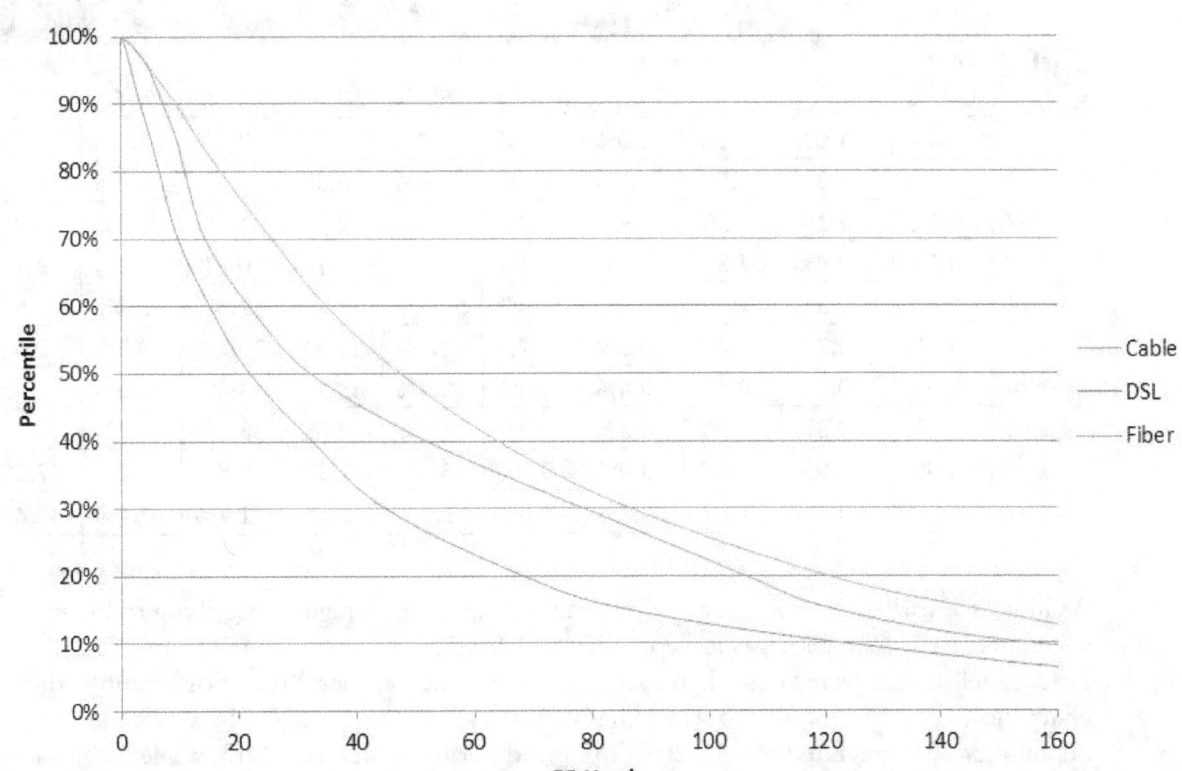

PANELIST MIGRATION

Of the 7,040 panelists who participated in the September 2012 study, 4,980 panelists continued to participate in the September 2013 study.[61] Figure 4 provides a percentage comparison of the 1,171 panelists who were part of the September 2012 study and migrated to a different speed tier between the September 2012 and September 2013 data collection periods. This table only includes panelists who were in both the September 2012 and September 2013 study. The highlighted boxes show the percentage of panelists who stayed in each tier from September 2012 to September 2013; the boxes to the left and right of those highlighted represent panelists who decreased or increased their speed, respectively, during this period.

Figure 4: Comparison of Panelist Population by Speed Tier – September 2012 and September 2013 Test Data.

2012 Range	2013 Range									
	0-1	1-3	3-7	7-10	10-15	15-20	20-25	25-30	30-50	50+
0-1	52.4%	31.0%	7.1%	0.0%	2.4%	2.4%	0.0%	2.4%	2.4%	0.0%
1-3	1.1%	71.3%	16.5%	1.1%	4.0%	2.9%	0.0%	0.7%	1.8%	0.4%
3-7	0.1%	2.1%	79.3%	1.9%	4.4%	4.5%	2.2%	2.9%	1.7%	0.9%
7-10	0.0%	2.4%	17.3%	62.2%	7.1%	0.8%	3.1%	0.8%	3.1%	3.1%
10-15	0.0%	0.3%	1.6%	0.5%	31.6%	55.5%	5.2%	2.4%	1.3%	1.5%
15-20	0.0%	0.2%	1.4%	0.2%	0.7%	41.3%	11.9%	26.7%	9.2%	8.4%
20-25	0.0%	0.0%	0.4%	0.4%	0.4%	9.7%	63.7%	4.4%	1.6%	19.4%
25-30	0.0%	0.3%	0.6%	0.3%	0.3%	4.5%	0.8%	38.6%	3.7%	51.0%
30-50	0.0%	0.0%	0.0%	0.0%	0.0%	3.1%	1.3%	0.8%	77.2%	17.6%
50+	0.0%	0.6%	1.1%	0.0%	0.6%	5.1%	2.3%	1.1%	1.7%	87.4%

As indicated earlier, panelists in September 2013 were, on average, subscribing to higher speed tiers than were panelists in September 2012. Chart 25 shows the percent of September 2012 panelists that were subscribed to a higher tier in September 2013. For example, the chart shows that 55.5 percent of the panelists subscribed to a 10-15 Mpbs service tier in September 2012 migrated to a 15-20 Mbps speed tier by September 2013, while 5.2% had migrated to a 20-25 Mbps speed tier. The largest increases can be observed in the 0-1 Mbps, 1 3 Mbps, 7 10 Mbps, and 25-30 Mbps tiers, where providers have made company-wide upgrades to subscriber tiers.[62] The tiers that panelists in the September 2012 study moved to in September 2013 are shown in Chart 26, and demonstrate that many subscribers moved to a tier in the next higher band.

Chart 25: Percent Change of September 2012 Panelists Subscribed to Higher Tier in September 2013

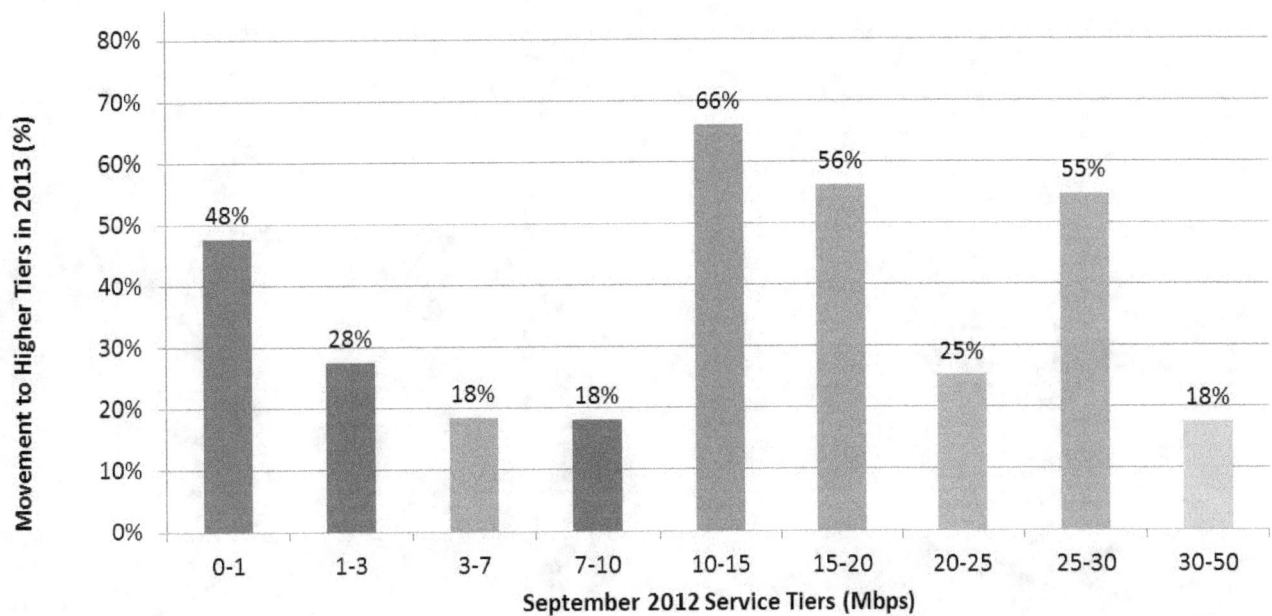

Chart 26: Percent Change of September 2012 Panelists Subscribed to Higher Tier in September 2013

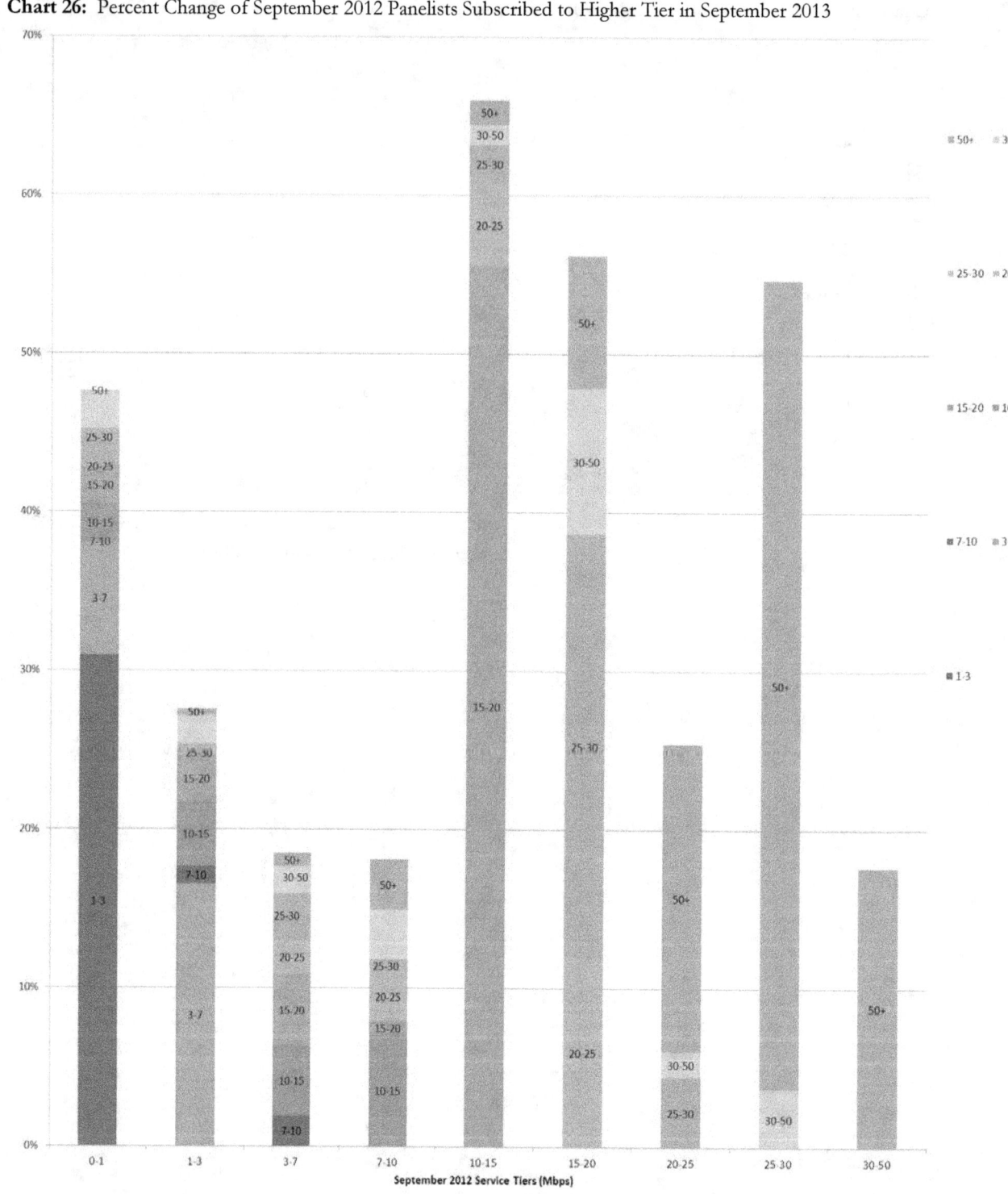

September 2012 Service Tiers (Mbps)

Conclusion and Next Steps

Consistent with recommendations in the National Broadband Plan, the FCC remains committed to working with stakeholders to develop awareness of broadband performance in an open and transparent environment. As described herein, this includes both moving forward with our existing program, as well as expanding to test and deliver information about additional broadband delivery technologies, including mobile broadband, to more comprehensively detail the consumer broadband experience. We plan to continue working with stakeholders to ensure that this program provides useful information.

Broadband Testing Program

The next testing period for this program is scheduled for September 2014, one year from the testing period analyzed in this Report. We anticipate that providers will continue to innovate and improve their offerings. We know based on stakeholder discussions that the major expansion in high speed service tiers first noted in the February 2013 Report was enabled by the cable industry's deployment of DOCSIS 3 technology which permitted service rates of 100 Mbps and above. The cable industry also has announced that it intends in the near future to extend its services to rates beyond 100 Mbps. Verizon fiber is now offering rates up to 500 Mbps in select parts of their market footprint, while Google offers 1 Gbps (1000 Mbps) service in Kansas City, MO and other areas. We recognize that the transition to higher speeds will not be without challenges. But our test results have consistently illustrated that subscribers to higher speed tiers generally use more data than other consumers and, thus, are immediately benefitting from these higher rates.

Launch of Measuring Broadband America: Mobile

After extensive discussions with the mobile broadband industry, we have committed to undertaking the first comprehensive public study of mobile broadband performance in the United States. Due to the dynamic nature of mobile network performance, this is a more complex undertaking than our fixed broadband measurement efforts. We expect the mobile efforts to evolve over time as we learn more about how these networks perform. We are grateful for the support we have received from industry in undertaking this effort. As with our efforts in the fixed broadband program, we believe working in partnership with stakeholders provides a better understanding of the challenges and results in a better product.

Measuring mobile broadband performance presents different technical challenges than fixed, and we are adapting our technology to these challenges. Consumers who volunteer for the program download an application onto their smartphones, which serves the same function that the Whitebox had in the fixed effort. We were pleased in November of 2013 to release our first app for Google Android based smartphones and in February of 2014 to release an app for the iPhone. We began collecting data based on these apps in November of 2013. We expect to release data associated with this program by no later than 2Q 2014.

Expanding Program to Include Targeted Studies of Specific Performance Metrics

As discussed in this Report, this program was initially focused on measuring broadband performance from the consumer to the end of the service provider's network. This simplified our initial task, and aligned with the service offerings provided by ISPs to consumers. However, Internet services and applications are supported by an end-to-end connection linking the application or service provider to the consumer in a complex and variable arrangement of interconnected networks. A consumer may virtually travel the globe in browsing the website of a company, news service, search engine, or government. Working with our partners, we continue to explore ways to leverage our measurement system to provide better information to consumers and more insights into the evolving performance of the Internet.

Commitment to Transparency

Both the Commission and SamKnows, the Commission's contractor for this program, recognize that, while the methodology descriptions included in this document provide an overview of the project as a whole, there will be a number of interested parties – ranging from recognized experts to members of the general public – who would be willing and to contribute to the project by reviewing the actual software used in the testing. SamKnows welcomes review of its software and technical platform, consistent with the Commission's goals of openness and transparency for this program.

All Data Released into the Public Domain

In the interest of transparency and to support additional research, the full Raw Bulk Data Set acquired during this study will be made available to the public.[63]

This Report, like the Reports that preceded it, could not have been produced without the ongoing discussions held with a broad array of individuals and entities, including the participating ISPs, equipment manufacturers, M-Lab, Level 3 Communications, and academics.

Acknowledgements

This Report benefited from the voluntary participation of a number of parties. The contribution of their expertise to this Report materially increased its quality. We would like to extend our thanks to the following entities:

- Adtran
- AT&T
- Cablevision Systems Corporation
- CenturyLink
- Charter Communications
- Comcast
- Corning
- Cox Communications
- Fiber to the Home Council
- Frontier Communications Company
- Georgia Institute of Technology
- Genband
- Insight Communications
- Intel
- Internet Society
- JDSU
- Level 3 Communications
- Mediacom Communications Corporation
- Massachusetts Institute of Technology
- M-Lab
- Motorola
- National Cable & Telecommunications Association
- New America Foundation
- Practicum Team, NCSU, Institute for Advanced Analytics
- Qwest Communications
- Time Warner Cable
- US Telecom Association
- Verizon
- ViaSat
- Windstream Communications

Finally, we again thank SamKnows for their performance during this endeavor, as they remain critical to this study's success.

Appendix A: Cable Providers DOCSIS Modem Disclosures

The following statements and disclosures were provided by various cable service providers to consumers to highlight the cable modem issue described above and raise consumer awareness of their upgrade policy:

CABLEVISION POLICY PROCESS REGARDING DOCSIS 1.1 AND 2.0 MODEMS

Over time Cablevision has increased speeds to enhance and improve its services. New equipment will sometimes be required to take full advantage of the increased speeds being delivered.

Details of the policies and procedures outlined below may change over time, but Cablevision will always take measures to keep customers aware of changes that may impact their service.

DOCSIS 1.1. Modems

To provide for a better customer experience, we have proactively notified and shipped a 3.0 modem to all customers with a 1.1 modem. Notification was sent via an email communication and an answering machine message. Modems are shipped via Federal Express and include detailed instructions on the proper installation of the modem. We continue to follow up with the small set of customers that have not yet swapped their 1.1 modem with the 3.0 modem.

DOCSIS 2.0 Modems

When a customer upgrades to Optimum Online Ultra 50 or Ultra 101, a check is performed to confirm the type of DOCSIS modem the customer currently has. Customers that have a 2.0 DOCSIS modem will be advised that a 3.0 DOCSIS modem is needed to enjoy the Ultra 50 or Ultra 101 speeds. Modems are shipped via Federal Express and include detailed instructions on the proper installation of the modem. We continue to follow up with the small set of customers that have not yet swapped their 2.0 modem with the 3.0 modem.

CHARTER COMMUNICATIONS LEGACY MODEM RESPONSE

Charter Communications provides high speed Internet to its customers in twenty-nine states. Over time we have continued to upgrade the Internet speeds we provide to our customers. As we have upgraded our network and provided faster speeds to our customers, Charter, like other high-speed broadband providers, has encountered existing modems that are not capable of utilizing the new, full speeds that Charter is making available and therefore need to be upgraded.

The use and presence of these legacy modems is likely to continue for the foreseeable future as there continue to be advances in the DOCSIS protocol that are allowing modems and cable networks to reach faster speeds. As Charter continues to deploy faster Internet speeds for the benefit of our customers, additional older modems will be limited by their embedded technology and unable of utilizing the capability of the new speed.

When an upgrade results in certain subscriber modems not being able to receive the faster speeds, Charter notifies those subscribers that they should upgrade, for free, to the latest generation modems so that they can take advantage of the superior broadband connection that we offer and have the best possible online experience. The type of notice has varied from emails to outbound telephone calls to messages in their monthly bills to a combination of these tactics. We explain to customers that *at no charge to them,* we will mail a new modem to their home or they can pick up a new device from one of our conveniently located retail stores. Each modem kit comes with easy to follow instructions on how to disconnect the old modem and start using the new modem. If customers prefer to have a new modem professionally installed by one of Charter's trained technicians, we will do so for a small fee.

While the details of exactly how we contact the customer and exactly what we say may change over time, it will always be our goal that our customers are aware of how to take advantage of the services we offer.

Finally, a current generation modem is included at no-cost in all of our service packages for new customers.

COMCAST MODEM UPGRADE PROCESS

At Comcast, providing great service for a great value is important. That is why we routinely increase the speeds we provide to our existing and new XFINITY Internet customers.

In order to enjoy the benefits of those speed increases customers occasionally will need new equipment. So Comcast has developed the Comcast Device Upgrade Portal – a place where customers who lease their cable modem from Comcast can easily request a replacement for their modem. Customers who own their modem may want to upgrade to a DOCSIS 3modem to receive the full range of speeds available with XFINITY Internet.

The Process

XFINITY ® customers who have leased modems and are identified as eligible for a modem replacement are notified in the following ways:

- Messages are included in the customer bill mailings, over multiple cycles, to ensure all affected customers are contacted
- Subsequently, letters are mailed to customers after a speed increase in the customer's region.
- Telephone calls are used to message customers after the above letter is mailed.
- A second round of telephone calls is used as a follow up.

XFINITY ® customers who own their modems receive the same notifications with an explanation of their modem replacement options.

XFINITY ® customers who lease their modem and receive the message are directed to visit the Comcast Device Upgrade Portal at:

www.comcast.com/deviceupgrade

Self-Service

XFINITY ® customers also have the ability to check the capability and compatibility of their modem online anytime at:

http://mydeviceinfo.comcast.net/

COX COMMUNICATIONS MODEM OUTREACH EFFORTS

Continuous network improvements allow Cox to enhance the speeds and reliability of our Internet service as well as offer additional value added features such as cloud storage, WiFi hotspots and security software. Cox increased speeds in all of its markets during 2013, with speeds increasing from 39% to as much as 200% in some markets.

Cox uses a variety of methods to communicate with its customers regarding the need for a modem capable of consistently delivering the broadband speeds associated with their particular package. Initially, at the time of Internet service subscription, the customer is advised which type of modem they will need for their package.

As package speeds are increased, customers receive notifications if their current modem is no longer sufficient for their new speeds. Cox uses multiple notification strategies, including emails to customers, bill messages and browser alerts. Cox also posts modem information on its support site located at http://ww2.cox.com/residential/support/internet/article.cox?articleId=d0168860-e4eb-11e0-dee8-000000000000.

TIME WARNER CABLE MODEM UPGRADE COMMUNICATIONS PROCESS

Time Warner Cable strives to offer customers fast and reliable Internet service, every step of the way. Customers have the option of leasing a modem from TWC, or buying their own modem. Leasing a modem from TWC is designed to ensure that customers have access to the right equipment for their Internet service level and speed. If a customer chooses to buy their own modem, TWC provides them with information about which modem is best for their TWC Internet service level and speed, and how to activate the modem once purchased, at www.twc.com/approvedmodems.

From time-to-time, Time Warner Cable initiates free speed upgrades to Internet service levels to thank its customers for their business. At times, these "customer appreciation" speed increases require the customer to upgrade their existing cable modem to take full advantage of the new Internet speed available to them. When this occurs, TWC provides targeted communications, in English and in Spanish where applicable, to inform the impacted customers that replacing their existing modem is recommended. These communications have typically involved:

- An **email** notifying the customer of the upcoming speed upgrade, and recommending an upgraded modem.
    - o Customers that lease their modems are directed to visit www.twc.com/modemswap, visit the closest Time Warner Cable store, or call us at 1-800-TWC-HELP (1-800-892-4357) to obtain an upgraded TWC-provided modem at no additional charge.
    - o Customers that own their own modem are directed to TWC's list of approved modems located at www.twc.com/approvedmodems to learn which type of modem is best for their Internet service level and speed.
- A **reminder email** within a short period of time to encourage customers to upgrade their modem and take advantage of the new speeds available to them, if they have not done so already.

In conjunction with the email communications described above, TWC has used a variety of other communication methods to encourage its customers to upgrade their modems, including postal letters, bill inserts, phone calls, voice blasts, and even print advertisements in local publications. TWC will continue to use these, and other, methods of communication to notify customers about speed increases and to encourage modem upgrades when needed.

Endnotes

[1] Our methodology permits either dropping up to five days during a test month or extending the test month into the following month to overcome network failures.

[2] ISP and provider are used interchangeably in this Report.

[3] Throughout this Report, observations on satellite technology are based on test results from ViaSat, which retails consumer broadband under the brand name Exede Internet.

[4] Satellites are commonly designated by the frequency band they use for communications. Ka band satellites operate in the frequency range of 26.5 GHz to 40 GHz. This frequency range is significantly higher than the older generation of satellites which operate at 12 GHz to 18 GHz and can more easily support higher capacities and speeds.

[5] See "Next Generation Satellite Broadband Passes Important Test," December 8, 2011, at http://www.telecompetitor.com/next-generation-satellite-broadband-passes-important-test (last accessed February 3, 2013).

[6] Measurement Lab (M-Lab) is an open, distributed server platform for researchers to deploy Internet measurement tools, http://www.measurementlab.net .

[7] As described more fully in the Technical Appendix, this study initially allowed for a target deployment in up to 10,000 homes across the United States, and the final volunteer pool was created from over 75,000 initial volunteer broadband subscribers.

[8] Testing for September 2013 started on September 16, 2013, and concluded on October 16, 2013.

[9] Participating ISPs were: AT&T (DSL); Cablevision (cable); CenturyLink (DSL); Charter (cable); Comcast (cable); Cox (cable); Frontier (DSL/fiber); Insight (cable); Mediacom (cable); Qwest (DSL); TimeWarner Cable (TWC) (cable); Verizon (DSL and fiber-to-the-home); Windstream (DSL); and ViaSat (satellite).

[10] Sustained speeds are described in the Technical Appendix and are averaged over five second intervals across the high and low rates that might dynamically occur in very short time interval measurements.

[11] ISPs typically advertise a small number of speed tiers but may also support legacy tiers that are no longer offered to new customers. As a result, a service provider may be required to support as many as ten service tiers at a given time.

[12] This limitation was a result of the finite number of measurement devices that could be deployed over the course of the project. Region-specific data would have required an order of magnitude or greater deployment of equipment, at a corresponding increase in cost.

[13] In 2012 the FCC and industry representatives jointly submitted proposals on broadband measurement technology to two standards organizations, the Internet Engineering Task Force (IETF) and the Broadband Forum, and also supported related work by the IEEE Computer Society. The goal of these proposals is to standardize broadband measurements as well as methods that would allow the more efficient collection of such data.

[14] See for example, http://hraunfoss.fcc.gov/edocs_public/attachmatch/FCC-12-90A1.pdf last access on 3/7/2014.

[15] Ex Parte, September 14, 2012, available at http://apps.fcc.gov/ecfs/document/view?id=7022016723

[16] Ex Parte, August 19, 2013, available at http://apps.fcc.gov/ecfs/document/view?id=7520939594

[17] See for example "Verizon blames Cogent for unbalanced peering in Netflix dispute", Fierce Telecom, http://www.fiercetelecom.com/story/verizon-blames-cogent-unbalanced-peering-netflix-dispute/2013-06-20

[18] See pg. 8 of the 2013 Report as well as endnote 14. http://www.fcc.gov/measuring-broadband-america/2012/july

[19] The Institute for Advanced Analytics had undertaken, at our invitation, an analysis of our test methodology and as part of their Report had suggested using this chart to better inform the consumer regarding the quality of their service, http://analytics.ncsu.edu .

[20] Qwest 40 Mbps; Comcast 50 Mbps; Time Warner Cable 50 Mbps; Verizon 50 Mbps; and Verizon Fiber 75 Mbps.

[21] Verizon Fiber 25 Mbps.

[22] The term "average" applied to results in this Report always means the arithmetic mean of the sample set under consideration. There is no weighting of samples.

[23] These are unweighted averages based on individual white boxes. However, white boxes are distributed across companies based on market share data provided to the FCC by each company on FCC Form 477 and based on direct communication between the FCC and individual companies. As a result, there is a close correlation between these unweighted averages and results that would be weighted by market share.

[24] A 24-hour average was computed each day and then averaged over Monday through Sunday.

[25] We made one change in presentation this year. In this Report, we decided to split Frontier into two categories, similar to what we have done for Verizon, i.e., Frontier-DSL and Frontier-fiber.

[26] When ViaSat is excluded from this calculation, this decrease becomes 3.6%.

[27] This is an unweighted average across all ISPs.

[28] With the exception of two providers, upload speeds during peak periods were 96 percent or better of advertised speeds.

[29] In this context, the closest server is the measurement server providing minimum round-trip time.

[30] This was calculated by taking an unweighted average of latency for cable, DSL, and fiber from the Latency sheet in the statistical averages test results.

[31] This was calculated by taking the percentage change of the unweighted average cable, DSL, and fiber 24 hour test results and the peak results for the same technologies in the statistical averages test results.

[32] For example, downloading a large file while browsing the web would limit the effectiveness of burst technology.

[33] As discussed later in the Report, due to latency concerns, the situation is more complex for

satellite.

[34] See, e.g., guidelines from Netflix support at
http://support.netflix.com/en/node/87#gsc.tab=0 (last accessed on January 1, 2013).

[35] Video content delivery companies are currently researching ultra-high definition video
services (e.g., 4K technology, which has a resolution of 12 Megapixels per frame, versus
present day 1080p High Definition television with a 2 Megapixel resolution), which would
require even higher transmission speeds.

[36] Daniel R. Glover, Hans Kruse, TCP Performance in a Geostationary Satellite Environment,
Annual Rev. of Comm. 1998, Int'l Eng. Consortium.

[37] With regard to latency, the International Telecommunications Union (ITU) has suggested
that one-way latency of less than 150 ms may affect some applications, while latency greater
than 400 ms is unacceptable for most uses of a broadband network. See
http://www.itu.int/rec/T-REC-G.114/en. While we found ViaSat to have a measured
one-way latency of 314 ms, this was for comparative purposes only and represented latency
only within the portion of the network that we test for all ISPs. We would expect end-to-
end latency to be somewhat higher due to a variety of factors.

[38] At the time of launch, this surpassed the total capacity of all satellites serving North
America. See "Viasat broadband 'super-satellite' launches" at
http://www.bbc.co.uk/news/science-environment-15358121 (last accessed January 30,
2013).

[39] For Viasat/Exede's service plans see: http://www.exede.com/internet-packages-
pricing/service-availability. One popular consumer activity, watching video over the
Internet, can consume as much as 1-2.8 GB/hour. See guidelines from Netflix support at
https://help.netflix.com/en/node/87. Thus, a single 2 hour movie could comprise 25 to
50 percent of a monthly data cap.

[40] In addition to the various data sets, the actual software code that was used for the testing
will be made available for academic and other researchers for non-commercial purposes.
To apply for non-commercial review of the code, interested parties may contact SamKnows
directly at team@samknows.com, with the subject heading "Academic Code Review."

[41] This data will be available when released through the FCC website at
http://www.fcc.gov/measuring-broadband-america.

[42] Actual information throughputs depend upon many factors, including transmission speed,
transport protocol characteristics, network status, and the capabilities of equipment sending
or receiving information across the network. At higher speeds, the interplay of these
factors becomes more evident.

[43] Latency is often colloquially called the "ping time," named after a network tool used to
measure the latency. The measurement methodology used in this Report differs slightly
from that tool, but measures the same round trip transit time between two points.

[44] See International Telecommunication Union (ITU), Series G: Transmission Systems and
Media, Digital Systems and Networks; International Telephone Connections and Circuits—
General Recommendations on the Transmission Quality for an Entire International
Telephone Connection, G.114 (May 2003).

[45] See, for example, Mark Claypool and Kajal Claypool, "Latency and player actions in online games", *Communications of the ACM*, vol. 49 (11), November 2006.

[46] As noted earlier, the full results of all 13 tests that were run in September 2013 are available at http://www.fcc.gov/measuring-broadband-america/2014.

[47] The September 2013 data set was validated to remove anomalies that would have produced errors in the Report. This data validation process is described in the Technical Appendix.

[48] Results from a particular company may include different technology platforms (e.g., results for Cox include both their DOCSIS 2 and DOCSIS 3 cable technologies; results for Verizon include both DSL and fiber). Throughout this Report, results are recorded separately for CenturyLink and Qwest. These two entities completed a merger on April 1, 2011; however, they continue to integrate operations through our 2013 testing and are identified separately as CenturyLink and Qwest/Centurylink.. References to Qwest/Centurylink in our charts are shortened to Qwest (CTL). Similarly, Insight Communications was acquired by Time Warner Cable on August 13, 2011. To ensure continuity of testing in September 2013, we continued to measure subscribers of the formerly distinct ISPs separately. We may revise this policy as these companies continue integration.

[49] All averages used in this Report are unweighted arithmetic averages of the relevant data sets. However, the sample plan was based on market share data for all ISPs. Comparison of unweighted averages with averages weighted by market share showed close agreement.

[50] A comparison of AT&T upload performance between this Report and the previous Reports identified a discrepancy in the February 2013 Report which showed an upload speed for AT&T at the 3 Mbps service tier of nearly 150 percent. The current Report shows an upload speed of 98 percent, which we believe to be correct and more accurate than the figure included in the previous Report. During the preparation of the February 2013 Report, we had failed to identify several consumers who had changed service providers and speed tiers.

[51] For example, AT&T has confirmed that they do not use this technology but their results exceeded the threshold set for this test.

[52] The FCC does not have detailed information on which speed tiers employ burst speed technology. This chart shows the percent difference between the sustained speed and bursts speed tests. Large differences in these speeds can be inferred as the result of burst speed technology being employed.

[53] We provide latency figures for peak periods. Latencies measured for other periods can be found in http://www.fcc.gov/measuring-broadband-america/2014/validated-data-fixed-2014#statisticalaverages.

[54] Due to the order of magnitude difference between terrestrial and satellite latencies, for clarity sake we choose not to include satellite latency in Chart 14.

[55] With the exception of ViaSat/Exede, all recorded latencies fall well under the maximum one-way latency of 150 ms recommended by the International Telecommunication Union (ITU).

[56] For a definition of web loading time, *see* Technical Appendix at pg. 23 at http://data.fcc.gov/download/measuring-broadband-america/2013/Technical-Appendix-feb-2013.pdf.

[57] For a discussion of the measurement devices used in this study, *see* Technical Appendix at 15-18. Although in throughout the Report we draw from test results from 6,493 panelists reporting in September 2013, some of the Whiteboxes were unable to collect byte count data, and consequently only results for Whiteboxes reporting these data are included in this measure.

[58] 1 terabyte is 1000000000000 bytes or 1000 gigabytes.

[59] The drop off for the 24 Mbps tier reflects the small number of volunteers participating in this study that were subscribed to this tier.

[60] In 2013 a total of 8,121,173,922 measurements were taken across 177,076,038 unique tests whereas in 2012 a total of 3,015,160,117 measurements were taken across 170,312,285 unique tests..

[61] Prior to the September 2013 testing period, 6,635 panelists from the February 2013 sample continued to supply data via their measurement devices. In addition, 405 subscribers were recruited after the February 2013 testing period, which brought the total subscribers reporting data in September 2013 to 7,040. After the data were processed, as discussed in more detail below, test results from a total of 6,733 panelists were used in the September 2013 Report.

[62] The speed tiers measured in the 2013 study are described in detail in the Technical Appendix at 28-29 at http://data.fcc.gov/download/measuring-broadband-america/2013/Technical-Appendix-feb-2013.pdf.

[63] Available at http://www.fcc.gov/measuring-broadband-america/2014/raw-data-fixed-2013.

www.ingramcontent.com/pod-product-compliance
Lightning Source LLC
Chambersburg PA
CBHW081252180526
45170CB00007B/2394